Στοιχείωσις θεολογική

PROCLUS'
ELEMENTS OF THEOLOGY

TRANSLATED BY
THOMAS TAYLOR

First Edition, 1816.

Re-printed with new formatting, 2017.

www.kshetrabooks.com

"The Elements of Theology", from
The Six Books of Proclus on the Theology of Plato
1st Edition, 1816

Re-print (with new formatting)

© Copyright 2017
All rights reserved.

ISBN: 978-1546304630

Foreword

This admirable work contains two hundred and eleven propositions, disposed in a scientific order, and supported by the firmest demonstrations. They begin from the super-essential unity, and proceed gradually through all the beautiful and wonderful progressions of divine causes, ending in the self-moving energies of souls. They possess all the accuracy of Euclid, and all the subtlety and sublimity necessary to a knowledge of the most profound theology; and may be considered as bearing the same relation to the Pythagoric and Platonic wisdom, as Euclid's Elements, to the most abstruse geometry. Patricius, the first Latin translator of this divine work, seems to have been very sensible of the truth of this observation: for he every where carefully distinguishes the propositions from their demonstrations; and adds the word 'corollary' to such consequencies as merit that appellation. His edition was published at Ferraria, 1583. quarto, under the title of Theological Elements. The Greek and Latin edition, is subjoined to Proclus's six books on Plato's Theology, Hamburgh, 1618. folio. (Thomas Taylor, from "Concerning the Published Writings of Proclus," from *The Philosophical and Mathematical Commentaries of Proclus on the First Book of Euclid's Elements, 1792.*)

I have already mentioned this admirable work, with the praise it so justly deserves, in my account of the life and writings of Proclus. I now add, with great pleasure that I have been no less fortunate with respect to the translation of these Elements than in translating the commentaries of Proclus. For the Greek text, is very frequently defective in parts essential to the meaning; and consequently necessary to the perfection of the whole. This defect I have been able to supply from the Latin version of Patricius, who appears to have had a perfect manuscript in his possession. But notwithstanding this assistance, I must freely own, that I never translated any thing which required so much intense thought, and severe labour in its execution. This indeed must necessarily be the case, if the abstruseness of the subject, the difficulty of finding proper terms, and the defects of the original, are properly considered. But the learned reader may be experimentally convinced of the truth of this assertion, if he only compares the Greek text with the Latin version of Æmilius Portus; in which I am sorry to say, he will scarcely find one proposition, in which Portus has not mistaken the sense of its author. Indeed were I disposed to entertain the critical reader, I might swell the volume with copious notes from the blunders of Portus; and display the superiority of my own version by contrasting the English with the Latin. But I consider verbose criticisms of this kind as both useless and pedantic; as remote from the philosophical genius; and as alone calculated to fill up the leisure hours of men, who have ruined their understandings in the study of words. The genuine Platonist who may be ignorant of Greek, will I persuade myself, rejoice to see this invaluable treasure in his native tongue; and those who have been led to consider the theology of the heathens as delusions, and absurdity, will doubtless be surprised to find, that it is replete with sublimest knowledge, and the most important truths. Yet I must admonish the reader, that these Elements cannot be understood by any one, who is not a thorough adept in Proclus' Commentaries on Euclid: for the propositions relate to the most abstract subjects that can be conceived; and the demonstrations are uncommonly subtle and profound. Indeed if opportunity permitted, I should attempt a commentary on every proposition; but this if ever I should be able to accomplish it, must be reserved for some more auspicious period. In the mean time, I hope that my occasional elucidations [see Taylor's notes], will be acceptable to the Platonic reader, and assist him in the study of this inestimable work. I only add, that these Elements form an admirable introduction to the six books of Proclus on Plato's Theology. (Thomas Taylor, introductory footnote to his first translation of the Elements of Theology, from *The Philosophical and Mathematical Commentaries of Proclus on the First Book of Euclid's Elements, 1792.*)

The Elements of Theology.

Proposition 1.

All multitude participates in a certain respect of *the one*.

For if it in no respect participates of *the one,* neither will the whole be one whole, nor each of the many of which the multitude consists; but there will also be a certain multitude arising from each of these, and this will be the case to infinity. Each of these infinites, likewise, will again be infinite multitude. For participating in no respect of any one, neither according to the whole of itself, nor according to each of the many which it contains, it will be in every respect, and according to the whole, infinite. For each of the many which you may assume, will either be one, or not one, will either be many or nothing. But if each is nothing, that also which consists of these will be nothing. And if each is many, each will consist of infinites infinitely: [and this not in capacity, but in energy]. These things, however, are impossible. For neither does any being consist of infinites infinitely assumed; since there is not more than the infinite; but that which consists of all is more than each. Nor is it possible for any thing to be composed from nothing. All multitude, therefore, participates in a certain respect of *the one*.

Proposition 2.

Every thing which participates of *the one,* is both one and not one.

For if it is not *the one* itself (since it participates of *the one*) being something else besides *the one*, it suffers, or is passive to it according to participation, and sustains to become one. If, therefore, it is nothing besides *the one,* it is one alone, and does not participate of *the one,* but will be *the one itself.* But if it is something besides *the one,* which is not *the one,* but its participant, it is both *not one,* and *one,* not indeed such a one as the one itself, but *one being,* as participating of *the one.* This, therefore, is not one, nor is it that which *the one* is. But it is one, and at the same time a participant of *the one.* Hence, being of itself not one, it is both one and not one, being something else besides *the one.* And so far indeed as it abounds, it is not one, but so far as it is passive [to the one] it is one. Every thing, therefore, which participates of *the one,* is both one, and not one.

Proposition 3.

Every thing which becomes one, becomes so through the participation of *the one,* and is one, so far as it suffers the participation of *the one.*

For if things which are not one become one, they doubtless become so by a conjunction and communication with each other, and they sustain the presence of *the one,* not being that which *the one itself* is. Hence, they participate of *the one* so far as they suffer to become one. For, if they are already one they will not become one; since that which is does not become that which it is already. But if they become one from nothing, *i.e.* from the privation of *the one,* since a certain one is ingenerated in them, *the one itself* is prior to them. [And this ingenerated one must be derived from *the one itself.* Every thing, therefore, which becomes one, becomes so through the participation of *the one,* etc.¹]

Proposition 4.

Every thing which is united is different from *the one itself.*

For if it is united, it will participate in a certain respect of *the one,* so far as it is said to be united. That, however, which participates of *the one,* is both one and not one. But *the one itself* is not both one and not one. For if this were the case, again the one which is in it would have both these, and this would take place to infinity, there being no *one itself* at which it is possible to stop; but every thing being one and not one, there will be something united which is different from *the one*. For if *the one* is the same with the united, it will be infinite multitude. And in a similar manner each of the things of which the united consists will be infinite multitude. [Every thing, therefore, which is united is different from *the one itself*.[2]]

Proposition 5.

All multitude is posterior to *the one*.

For if multitude is prior to *the one, the one* indeed will participate of multitude, but multitude which is prior to *the one* will not participate of *the one,* since that multitude existed prior to the subsistence of *the one*. For it will not participate of that which is not; because that which participates of *the one*, is one and at the same time not one; but *the one* will not yet subsist, that which is first being multitude. It is, however, impossible that there should be a certain multitude, which in no respect whatever participates of *the one*. Multitude, therefore, is not prior to *the one*.

But if multitude subsists simultaneously with *the one,* and they are naturally coordinate with each other; for nothing of time will prevent them being so; neither will *the one* of itself be many, nor will multitude be one, as being at one and the same time oppositely divided by nature, if neither is prior or posterior to the other. Hence, multitude of itself will not be one, and each of the things that are in it will not be one, and this will be the case to infinity, which is impossible. Multitude, therefore, according to its own nature, participates of *the one,* and it will not be possible to assume any thing of it which is not one. For not being one, it will be an infinite consisting of infinites, as has been demonstrated. Hence, it entirely participates of *the one*. If, therefore, *the one* which is of itself one, in no respect participates of multitude, multitude will be entirely posterior to *the one;* participating indeed of *the one,* but not being participated by *the one*.

But if *the one* also participates of multitude, subsisting indeed as one according to hyparxis, but as not one, according to participation, *the one* will be multiplied, just as multitude is united on account of *the one. The one,* therefore, will communicate with multitude, and multitude with *the one*. But things which coalesce, and communicate in a certain respect with each other, if indeed they are collected together by something else, that something else is prior to them. But if they themselves collect themselves, they are not opposed to each other. For opposites do not hasten to each other. Hence, if *the one* and multitude are oppositely divided, and multitude so far as multitude is not one, and *the one* so far as one is not multitude, neither will one of these subsisting in the other be one and at the same time two. If, also, there is something prior to them which collects them, this will either be one, or not one. But if it is not one, it will either be many or nothing. It will not however be many, lest multitude should be prior to *the one,* nor yet will it be nothing. For how can nothing congregate? It is, therefore, one alone. For this which is the one cannot be many, lest there should be a progression to infinity. It is, therefore, *the one itself,* and all multitude is from *the one itself.*

Proposition 6.

Concerning Unity.

Every multitude consists either of things united, or of unities.

For that each of things many will not be itself multitude alone, and again that each part of this will not be multitude alone is evident. But if it is not multitude alone, it is either united, or unities (εναδες). And if, indeed, it participates of *the one* it is united; but if it consists of things of which that which is primarily united consists, it will be unities. For if there is *the one itself,* there is also that which primarily participates of it, and which is primarily united. But this consists of unities. For if it consists of things united, again things united consist of certain things, and this will be the case to infinity. It is necessary, however, that what is primarily united should consist of unities. And thus we have discovered what we proposed at first, (*viz.* that every multitude consists either of things united, or of unities.]

Proposition 7.

Concerning producing causes and things produced.

Every thing productive of another is more excellent than the nature of the thing produced.

For it is either more excellent, or less excellent, or equal. Hence, that which is produced from this, will either also itself possess a power productive of something else, or it will be entirely unprolific. But if it it unprolific, according to this very thing it will be inferior to that by which it was produced. And through its inefficacy it is unequal to its cause which is prolific, and has the power of producing. But if it also is productive of other things, it either likewise produces that which is equal to itself, and this in a similar manner in all things, and all beings will be equal to each other, and no one thing will be better than another, that which produces, always giving subsistence in a consequent series to that which is equal to itself; or it produces that which is unequal to itself, and thus that which is produced, will no longer be equal to that which produces it. For it is the province of equal powers to produce equal things. The progeny of these, however, will be unequal to each other, if that which produces indeed, is equal to the cause prior to itself, but the thing posterior to it is unequal to it. Hence, it is not proper that the thing produced should be equal to its producing cause.

Moreover, neither will that which produces ever be less than that which is produced by it. For if it imparts essence to the thing produced, it will also supply it with essential power. But if it is productive of all the power which that posterior to it possesses, it will also be able to produce itself such as that posterior nature is. And if this be the case it will also make itself[3] more powerful. For impotency cannot hinder, productive power being present, nor a defect of will; since all things naturally aspire after good. Hence, if it is able to render another thing more perfect, it will also perfect itself before it perfects that which is posterior to itself. Hence, that which is produced, is not equal to, nor more excellent than, its producing cause. The producing cause, therefore, is in every respect better than the nature of the thing produced.

Proposition 8.

Concerning the first good, which is called the good itself.

That which is primarily good, and which is no other than *the good itself* is the leader of all things that in any way whatever participate of good.

For if all beings aspire after good, it is evident that what is primarily good is beyond beings. For if it is the same with some one being, either being and *the good* are the same, and this particular being will no longer be desirous of good, since it is that to which it is passive, [*i.e.* since it is *the good*]. For that which aspires after any thing is indigent of that after which it aspires, and is different from it. And [if some one being and *the good* are the same] being indeed will participate, and that which is participated in being will be *the good*. Hence, *the good* is a certain good inherent in a certain participant, and after which the participant alone aspires, but is not that which is simply good, and which all beings desire. For this is the common object of desire to all beings. But that which is inherent in a certain thing, pertains to that alone which participates of it. Hence, that which is primarily good, is nothing else than good. For whatever else you may add to it, you will diminish by the addition *the good,* and will make it to be a certain good, instead of that which is simply good. For that which is added not being *the good,* but something less than it, will by its own essence diminish *the good.*

Proposition 9.

Concerning that which is sufficient to itself.

Every thing which is sufficient to itself, either according to essence, or according to energy, is more excellent than that which is not sufficient to itself, but has the cause of its perfection suspended from another cause.

For if all beings naturally aspire after good, and one thing supplies well-being from itself,[4] but another is indigent of something else, the one indeed will have the cause of good present, but the other separate and apart. By how much the nearer, therefore, the former is to that which supplies the object of desire [*i.e.* to *the good*], by so much the more excellent will it be than that which is indigent of a separate cause, and externally receives the perfection of its hyparxis, or its energy. For since that which is sufficient to itself is both similar and diminished, it is more similar to *the good itself* [than that which is not self-sufficient]. It is diminished indeed through participating of *the good,* and because it is not primarily *the good.* Yet it is in a certain respect allied to it, so far as it is able to possess good from itself. But to participate, and to participate through another, are more remote from that which is primarily good, and which is nothing else than good.

Proposition 10.

Every thing which is sufficient to itself is inferior to that which is simply good.

For what else is a thing sufficient to itself, than that which from itself and in itself possesses good? But this is now full of good, and participates of it, but is not that which is simply good. For that is better than participation and plenitude, as has been demonstrated. If, therefore, that which is sufficient to itself, fills itself with good, that from which it fills itself, will be more excellent than the self-sufficient, and will be above self-sufficiency. And neither will that which is simply good be indigent of any thing. For it does not aspire after any thing else; since by aspiring after it would be deficient of good. Nor is that which is simply good sufficient to itself. For thus it would be full of good, and would not be primarily the good.

Proposition 11.

Concerning Cause.

All beings proceed from one first cause.

For either there is not any cause of beings, or the causes of all finite things are in a circle, or the ascent is to infinity, and one thing is the cause of another, and the pre-subsistence of essence will in no respect stop. If, however, there is no cause of beings, there will neither be an order of things second and first, of things perfecting and perfected, of things adorning and adorned, of things generating and generated, and of agents and patients, nor will there be any science of beings. For the knowledge of causes is the work of science, and we are then said to know scientifically, when we know the causes of things.[5]

But if causes revolve in a circle, the same things will be prior and posterior, more powerful and more imbecil. For every thing which produces is better than the nature of that which is produced. It makes, however, no difference to conjoin cause to effect, and to produce from cause, through many, or through fewer media. For cause will be more excellent than all the intermediate natures of which it is the cause. And by how much the more numerous the media, by so much greater is the causality of the cause.

And if the addition of causes is to infinity, and there is always again another cause prior to another, there will be no science of any being. For there is not a knowledge of any thing infinite. But causes being unknown, neither will there be a science of the things consequent to the causes. If, therefore, it is necessary that there should be a cause of beings, and causes are distinct from the things caused, and there is not an ascent to infinity, there is a first cause of beings, from which as from a root every thing proceeds; some things indeed being nearer to, but others more remote from it. For that it is necessary there should be one principle has been demonstrated;[6] because all multitude subsists posterior to *the one*.

Proposition 12.

The principle and first cause of all beings is *the good*.

For if all things proceed from one cause, [as has been above demonstrated] it is requisite to call that cause either *the good,* or that which is more excellent than *the good*. But if it is more excellent than *the good,* whether is any thing imparted by it to beings, and to the nature of beings, or nothing? And if indeed nothing is imparted by it an absurdity will ensue. For we shall no longer preserve it in the order of cause; since it is every where requisite that something should be present from cause to things caused,[7] and especially from the first cause from which all things are suspended, and on account of which every being exists. But if something is imparted by it to beings, in the same manner as there is by *the good,* there will be something better than goodness in beings imparted to them by the first cause. For being more excellent than, and above *the good,* it can never bestow on secondary natures any thing subordinate to that which is imparted by the nature posterior to itself.[8] But what can be more excellent than goodness? Since we say that the more excellent itself is that which participates of a greater good. Hence, if that which is not good cannot be said to be more excellent than, it must entirely be secondary to *the good*. If, likewise, all beings aspire after *the good,* how is it any longer possible that there should be something prior to this cause? For if they also aspire after that which is prior to *the good,* how can they especially aspire after *the good?* But if they do not aspire after it, how is it possible that things which proceed from it should not desire the cause of all? Hence, if it is *the good* from which all beings are suspended, *the good* is the principle and first cause of all things.

Proposition 13.

Every good has the power of uniting its participants, and every union is good; and *the good* is the same with *the one.*

For if *the good* is preservative of all beings, (on which account also it is desirable to all things) but that which is preservative and connective of the essence of every thing, is *the one;* for all things are preserved by *the one,* and dispersion removes every thing from essence;—if this be the case, *the good* will cause those things to which it is present, to be one, and will connect and contain them according to union. And if *the one* is collective and connective of beings, it will perfect every thing by its presence. Hence, therefore, it is good to all things to be united. If, however, union is of itself good, and good has the power of uniting, the simply good, and the simply one are the same, uniting and at the same time benefiting beings. Hence it is that those things which after a manner fall off from *the good,* are at the same time also deprived of the participation of *the one.* And those things which become destitute of *the one,* being filled with separation, are after the same manner likewise deprived of *the good.* Hence, goodness is union, and union is goodness, and *the one* is that which is primarily good.

Proposition 14.

Concerning the immoveable and self-motive principle, or cause.

Every being is either immoveable or moved. And if moved, it is either moved by itself, or by another. And if indeed it is moved by itself, it is self-motive; but if by another, it is alter-motive. Every thing therefore, is either immoveable, or self-motive, or alter-motive.

For it is necessary since there are alter-motive natures, that there should also be that which is immoveable, and that the self-motive nature should subsist between these. For if every thing alter-motive is moved in consequence of being moved by another thing, motions will either be in a circle, or they will proceed to infinity.[9] But they will neither be in a circle, nor have an infinite progression, since all beings are bounded by the principle of things and that which moves is better than that which is moved. Hence there will be something immoveable which first moves.[10] But if this be the case, it is also necessary that there should be something which is self-motive. For if[11] all things should stop, what will that be which is first moved? It cannot be that which is immoveable;[12] for it is not naturally adapted to be moved; nor that which is alter-motive; for that is moved by something else. It remains therefore, that the self-motive nature is that which is primarily moved. For it is this also which conjoins alter-motive natures to that which is immoveable, being in a certain respect a middle, moving and at the same time being moved. For of these, the immoveable moves only, but the alter-motive is moved only. Every thing therefore, is either immoveable, or self-motive, or alter-motive.

Corollary.

From these things likewise, it is evident, that of things which are moved, the self-motive nature is the first; but that of things which move the immoveable is the first.

Proposition 15.

Concerning an incorporeal essence, and that the peculiarity of it it.

Every thing which is converted to itself is incorporeal.

For no body is naturally adapted to revert to itself. For if that which is converted to any thing is conjoined with that to which it is converted, it is evident that all the parts of the body which is converted to itself, will be conjoined with all the parts. For this it is for a thing to be converted to itself, when both that which is converted, and that to which it is converted, become one. This however is impossible in body, and in short, in all partible things. For the whole of that which is partible is not conjoined with the whole, on account of the separation of the parts, some of which are situated differently from others. No body therefore, is naturally adapted to revert to itself, so as that the whole may be converted to the whole. Hence if there is any thing which has the power of reverting to itself, it is incorporeal and impartible.

Proposition 16.

Every thing which is converted to itself, has an essence separate from all body.

For if it was inseparable from any body whatever, it would not have a certain energy separate from body.[13] For thus energy would be more excellent than essence; since the latter indeed would be indigent of bodies, but the former would be sufficient to itself, and would not be in want of bodies: If therefore any thing is essentially inseparable from body, it is also in a similar manner inseparable according to energy, or rather it is in a still greater degree inseparable. But if this be the case, it will not revert to itself. For that which is converted to itself being something different from body, has an energy separate from body, and not either through, or together with body, since the energy, and that to which the energy is directed, are not at all in want of body. Hence, that which is converted to itself, is entirely separate from bodies.

Proposition 17.

Every thing which moves itself primarily, is convertive to itself.

For if it moves itself, and its motive energy is directed to itself, that which moves and that which is moved are at the same time one. For it either moves in a part but is moved in a part, or the whole moves and is moved, [or the whole moves, but a part is moved, or[14]] the contrary. But if one part indeed, is that which moves, and another part is that which is moved, it will not be essentially self-motive, since it will consist of things which are not self-motive, but which appear indeed to be so, yet are not so essentially.

If however, the whole moves, but the part is moved, or the contrary, there will be a certain part in both which according to one, moves and at the same time is moved.[15] And this is that which is primarily self-motive. If however, one and the same thing moves and is moved, it will have the energy of moving to itself, being motive of itself. But it is converted to that towards which it energizes. Every thing therefore which primarily moves itself, is converted to itself.

Proposition 18.

Every thing which imparts existence to others, is itself that primarily which it communicates to the natures that are supplied by it with existence.

For if it gives existence, and makes the communication from its own essence, that which it gives is subordinate to its own essence [by the 7th Proposition]. But that which it is, it is in a greater and more perfect degree; since every thing which gives subsistence to a certain thing, is better than and not the same with it. For it is primarily, but the other is secondarily that which it is. For it is necessary either that each should be the same, and that there should be one definition of both, or that there should be nothing common and the same in both, or that the one should subsist primarily, but the other secondarily. If however indeed, there is the same definition of both, the one will no longer be cause, but the other effect; nor will the one subsist essentially, but the other by participation; nor will the one be the maker, but the other the thing made. But if they have nothing which is the same, the one will not give subsistence to the other by its very being, in consequence of communicating nothing to the existence of the other. Hence, it remains that the one should be primarily that which it gives, but that the other should be secondarily that to which existence is given; the former supplying the latter from its very being.

Proposition 19.

Every thing which is primarily inherent in a certain nature of beings, is present to all the beings that are arranged according to that nature, and this conformably to one reason, and after the same manner.

For if it is not present to all of them after the same manner, but to some and not to others, it is evident that it was not primarily in that nature, but that it is in some things primarily, and in others secondarily, that sometimes participate of it. For that which at one time exists, but at another time does not, does not exist primarily, nor of itself. But it is adventitious, and is imparted from some other place to the things in which it is thus inherent.

Proposition 20.

The essence of soul is beyond all bodies, the intellectual nature is beyond all souls, and *the one* is beyond all intellectual hypostases.

For every body is moveable by something else, but is not naturally adapted to move itself, but by the presence of soul is moved of itself, lives on account of soul, and when soul is present, is in a certain respect self-moveable, but when it is absent is alter-moveable, as deriving this nature from soul which is allotted a self-moveable essence. For to whatever nature soul is present, to this it imparts self-motion. It is however, by a much greater priority that which it imparts by its very being. Hence, it is beyond bodies, which become self-movable by participation as being essentially self-moveable.

Again however, soul which is moved from itself, has an order secondary to the immoveable nature, which subsists immoveable according to energy. Because of all the natures that are moved, the self-moveable essence is the leader; but of all that move, the immoveable is the leader. If therefore soul being moved from itself, moves other things, it is necessary that prior to it, there should be that which moves immovably But intellect moves being immoveable, and energizing always with an invariable sameness of subsistence. For soul on account of intellect participates of perpetual intellectual energy, just as body on account of soul possesses the power of moving itself. For if perpetual intellection was primarily in soul, it would be inherent in all souls, in the same manner as the self-motive power. Hence, perpetual intellection is not primarily in soul. It is necessary therefore, that prior to it, there should be that which is primarily intellective. And hence, intellect is prior to souls.

Moreover, *the one* is prior to intellect. For intellect though it is immoveable yet is not *the one;* for it intellectually perceives itself, and energizes about itself. And of *the one* indeed, all beings in whatever way they may exist, participate; but all beings do not participate of intellect. For those beings to whom intellect is present by participation, necessarily participate of knowledge; because intellectual knowledge is the principle and first cause of the gnostic energy. *The one* therefore, is beyond intellect; and there is no longer any thing else beyond *the one*.

For *the one* and *the good* are the same. But *the good*, as has been demonstrated, is the principle of all things.

Proposition 21.

That intellect is not the first cause.

Every order beginning from a monad, proceeds into a multitude coordinate to the monad, and the multitude of every order is referred to one monad.

For the monad having the relation of a principle, generates a multitude allied to itself. Hence one series, and one whole order has a decrement into multitude from the mound. For there would no longer be an order, or a series, if the monad remained of itself unprolific. But multitude is again referred to the one common cause of all coordinate natures. For that in every multitude which is the same, has not its progression from one of those things of which the multitude consists. For that which subsists from one alone of the many, is not common to all, but eminently possesses the peculiarity of that one alone. Hence, since in every order there is a certain communion, connexion, and sameness, through which some things are said to be coordinate, but others of a different order, it is evident that sameness is derived to every order from one principle.[16] In each order, therefore, there is one monad prior to the multitude, which imparts one ratio and connexion to the natures arranged in it, both to each other, and to the whole.

For let one thing be the cause of another, among things that are under the same series: but that which ranks as the cause of the one series, must necessarily be prior to all in that series, and all things must be generated by it at coordinate, not so that each will be a certain particular thing, but that each will belong to this order.

Corollary.

From these things it is evident that both unity and multitude are inherent in the nature of body; that one nature has many natures co-suspended from it; and that many natures proceed from the one nature of the universe. It follows also, that the order of souls originates from one first soul, and proceeds with diminution into the multitude of souls. That in the intellectual essence also, there is an intellectual monad; and that a multitude of intellects proceeds from one intellect, and is converted to it. That a multitude of unities likewise originates from *the one* which is prior to all things; and that there is an extension of these unities to *the one*. Hence, after the first one there are unities; after the first intellect, there are intellects; after the first soul there are souls; and after total nature, there are natures.

Proposition 22.

Every thing which subsists primarily and principally in each order is one, and is neither two, nor more than two, but is only begotten.

For, if it be possible, let there be two things which thus subsist; since there will be the same impossibility if there are more than two; or let that which subsists primarily consist of both these. But if indeed it consists of both, it will again be one, and there will not be two things that are first. And if it be one of the two, each will not be first. Nor if both are equally primary, will each have a principal subsistence. For if one of them is primary, but this is not the same with the other, what will it be in that order? For that subsists primarily, which is nothing else than that which it is said to be. But each of these being different is, and at the same time is not that which it is said to be.

If, therefore, these differ from each other, but they do not primarily differ so far as they are that which they are said to be; for this primarily suffers that which is the same; both will not be first, but that of which both participating, are said to subsist primarily.

Corollary.

From these things it is evident, that what is primarily being is one alone, and that there are not two primary beings, or more than two; that the first intellect is one alone, and that there are not two first intellects; and that the first soul is one. This is also the case with every form, such as the primarily beautiful, and the primarily equal. And in a similar manner in all things. Thus also, with respect to the form of animal, and the form of man, the first of each is one; for the demonstration is the same.

Proposition 23.

Concerning the Imparticipable.[17]

Every imparticipable gives subsistence from itself to things which are participated. And all participated hypostases are extended to imparticipable hyparxes.

For that which is imparticipable having the relation of a monad, as subsisting from itself, and not from another, and being exempt from participants, generates things which are able to be participated. For either[18] it remains of itself barren, and possesses nothing honourable; or it gives something from itself. And that which receives indeed from it participates, but that which is given subsists in a participated manner. But every thing which is something belonging to a certain thing by which it is participated,[19] is secondary to that which is similarly present to all things, and which fills all things from itself. For that which is in one thing is not in others. But that which is similarly present to all things, in order that it may illuminate all things, is not in one thing, but is prior to all things. For it is either in all things, or in one of all, or it is prior to all. But that indeed which is in all things being distributed into all, will again require another thing which may unite that which is distributed. And all things will no longer participate of the same thing, but this of one thing, and that of another, the one being divided. But if it is in one of all things, it will no longer be common to all, but to one thing. Hence if it is common to things able to participate, and is common to all, it will be prior to all. But this is imparticipable.

Proposition 24.

Every thing which participates is inferior to that which is participated; and that which is participated is inferior to that which is imparticipable.

For that which participates, being imperfect prior to participation, but becoming perfect through participation, is entirely secondary to that which is participated, so far as it is perfect by participating. For so far as it was imperfect, it is inferior to that which it participates, which makes it to be perfect. That however which is participated since it belongs to a certain thing, and not to all things, is again allotted an hyparxis subordinate to that which is something belonging to all things, and not to a certain thing. For the latter is more allied to the cause of all; but the former is less allied to it.

The imparticipable, therefore, is the leader of things which are participated; but the latter are the leaders of participants. For, in short, the imparticipable is one prior to the many; but that which is participated in the many, is one and at the same time not one; and every thing which participates is not one, and at the same time one.

Proposition 25.

Concerning the Perfect.

Every thing perfect proceeds to the generation of those things which it is able to produce, imitating the one principle of all.

For as that on account of its own goodness, unically gives subsistence to all beings; for *the good* and *the one* are the same, so that the boniform is the same with the unical; thus also those things which are posterior to the first, on account of their perfection, hasten to generate beings inferior to their own essence. For perfection is a certain portion of *the good,* and the perfect, so far as it is perfect, imitates *the good*. But *the good* gives subsistence to all things. So that the perfect likewise, is productive according to nature of those things which it is able to produce. And that indeed which is more perfect, by how much the more perfect it is, by so much the more numerous are the progeny of which it is the cause. For that which is more perfect, participates in a greater degree of *the good*. It is, therefore, nearer to *the good*. But this being the case, it is nearer to the cause of all. And thus, it is the cause of a greater number of effects. That, however, which is more imperfect, by how much the more imperfect it is, by so much the less numerous are the effects of which it is the cause. For being more remote from that which produces every thing, it gives subsistence to fewer effects. For to that which gives subsistence to, or adorns, or perfects, or connects, or vivifies, or fabricates, all things, that nature is more allied which produces a greater number of each of these; but that is more remote which produces a less number of each.

Corollary.

From these things it is evident, that the nature which is most remote from the principle of all, is unprolific, and is not the cause of any thing. For if it generated a certain thing, and had something posterior to itself, it is evident that it would no longer be most remote, but that which it produced would be more remote than itself, from the principle of all things, but it would be nearer to productive power, and besides[20] this, would imitate the cause which is productive of all beings.

Proposition 26.

Every cause which is productive of other things, itself abiding in itself, produces the natures posterior to itself, and such as are successive.

For if it imitates *the one,* but that immovably gives subsistence to things posterior to itself, every thing which produces will possess in a similar manner the cause of productive energy. But *the one* gives subsistence to things immovably For if through motion, the motion will be in it, and being moved, it will no longer be *the one,* in consequence of being changed from *the one*. But if motion subsists together with it, it will also be from *the one,* and either there will be a progression to infinity, or *the one* will produce immovably; and every thing which produces will imitate the producing cause of all things. For every where, from that which is primarily, that which is not primarily derives its subsistence; so that the nature which is productive of certain things originates from that which is productive of all things. Hence every producing cause produces subsequent natures from itself. And while productive natures abide in themselves undiminished, secondary natures are produced from them. For that which is in any respect diminished, cannot abide such as it is.

Proposition 27.

Every producing cause, on account of its perfection, and abundance of power, is productive of secondary natures.

For if it produced not on account of the perfect, but through a defect according to power, it would not be able to preserve its own order immoveable. For that which imparts existence to another thing through defect and imbecility, imparts subsistence to it, through its own mutation and change in quality. But every thing which produces remains such as it is, and in consequence of thus remaining, that which is posterior to it[21] proceeds into existence. Hence, being full and perfect, it gives subsistence to secondary natures immovably and without diminution, it being that which it is, and neither being changed into them, nor diminished. For that which is produced, is not a distribution into parts of the producing cause; since this is neither appropriate to the generating energy, nor to generating causes. Nor is it a transition. For it does not become the matter of that which proceeds; since it remains such as it is, and that which is produced is different from it. Hence that which generates is firmly established undiminished; through prolific power multiplies itself and from itself imparts secondary hypostases.

Proposition 28.

Every producing cause gives subsistence to things similar to itself, prior to such as are dissimilar.

For since that which produces is necessarily more excellent than that which is produced, they can never be simply the same with each other, and equal in power. But if they are not the same and equal, but different and unequal, they are either entirely separated from each other, or they are both united and separated. If, however, they are entirely separated, they will not accord with each other, and no where will that which proceeds from a cause sympathize with it. Hence neither will one of these participate of the other, being entirely different from it. For that which is participated, gives communion to its participant, with reference to that of which it participates. Moreover, it is necessary that the thing caused should participate of its cause, as from thence possessing its essence.

But if that which is produced, is partly separated from and party united to its producing cause, if indeed, it suffers each of these equally, it will equally participate and not participate. So that after the same manner, it will both have essence and not have it from the producing cause. And if it is more separated from than united to it, the thing generated will be more foreign than allied to that by which it is generated, will be more unadapted than adapted to it, and be more deprived of, than possess sympathy with it. If, therefore, the things which proceed from causes are allied to them according to their very being, have sympathy with them, are naturally suspended from them, and aspire after contact with them, desiring good, and obtaining the object of their desire through the cause of their existence,—if this be the case, it is evident that things produced are in a greater degree united to their producing causes, than separated from them. Things, however, which are more united, are more similar than dissimilar to the natures to which they are especially united. Every producing cause, therefore, gives subsistence to things similar to itself prior to such as are dissimilar.

Proposition 29.

Every progression is effected through a similitude of secondary to first natures.

For if that which produces, gives subsistence to similars prior to dissimilars, the similitude derived from the producing causes will give subsistence to the things produced. For similars are rendered similar through similitude, and not through dissimilitude. If, therefore, progression in its diminution preserves a [certain] sameness of that which is generated with that which generates, and exhibits that which is posterior to the generator such in a secondary degree, as the generator is primarily, it will have its subsistence through similitude.

Proposition 30.

Every thing which is produced from a certain thing without a medium, abides in its producing cause, and proceeds from it.

For if every progression is effected, while primary natures remain permanent, and is accomplished through similitude, similars being constituted prior to dissimilars,—if this be the case, that which is produced will in a certain respect abide in its producing cause. For that which entirely proceeds, will have nothing which is the same with the abiding cause, but will be perfectly separated from it, and will not have any thing common with and united to it. Hence it will abide in its cause, in the same manner as that also abides in itself. If, however, it abides, but does not proceed, it will in no respect differ from its cause, nor will it, while that abides, be generated something different from it. For if it is something different it is separated and apart from its cause. If, however, it is apart, but the cause abides, it will proceed from the cause, in order that while it abides, it may be separated from it. So far therefore, as that which is produced has something which is the same with the producing[22] cause, it abides in it; but so far as it is different, it proceeds from it. Being, however, similar, it is in a certain respect at once both the same and different. Hence, it abides, and at the same time proceeds, and it is neither of these without the other.

Proposition 31.

Every thing which proceeds from a certain thing essentially, is converted to that from which it proceeds.

For if it should proceed indeed, but should not return to the cause of this progression, it would not aspire after its cause. For every thing which desires is converted to the object of its desire. Moreover, everything aspires after good, and to each thing the attainment of it is through the proximate cause. Every thing, therefore, aspires after its cause. For well-being is derived to every thing from that through which its existence is derived. But appetite is first directed to that through which well-being is derived. And conversion is to that to which appetite is first directed.

Proposition 32.

All conversion is effected through the similitude of the things converted to that to which they are converted.

For every thing which is converted, hastens to be conjoined with its cause,[23] and aspires after communion and colligation with it. But similitude binds all things together, just as dissimilitude separates and disjoins all things. If, therefore, conversion is a certain communion and contact, but all communion and all contact are through similitude,— if this be the case, all conversion will be effected through similitude.

Proposition 33.

Every thing which proceeds from a certain thing and is converted to it, has a circular energy.

For if it reverts to that from which it proceeds, it conjoins the end to the beginning, and the motion is one and continued; one motion being from that which abides, but the other being directed to the abiding cause. Hence all things proceed in a circle from causes to causes; greater and less circles being continually formed of conversions, some of which are to the natures [immediately] placed above the things that are converted, but others are to still higher natures, and so on as far as to the principle of all things. For all things proceed from this principle, and are converted to it.

Proposition 34.

Every thing which is converted according to nature, makes its conversion to that, from which also it had the progression of its proper hypostasis.

For if it is converted according to nature, it will have an essential desire of that to which it is converted. But if this be the case, the whole being of it is suspended from that to which it makes an essential conversion, and it is essentially similar to it. Hence also it has a natural sympathy with, as being allied to the essence of it. If this, however, be the case, either the being of both is the same, or the one is derived from the other, or both are allotted similitude from a certain other one. But if the being of both is the same, how is the one naturally converted to the other? And if both are from a certain one, it will be according to nature for both to be converted to that one. It remains, therefore, that the one must derive its being from the other. But if this be the case, the progression will be from that to which the conversion is according to nature.

Corollary.

From these things, therefore, it is evident that intellect is the object of desire to all things, that all things proceed from intellect, and that the whole world though it is perpetual possesses its essence from intellect. For it is not prevented from proceeding from intellect because it is perpetual. For neither because it is always arranged is it not converted to intellect, but it always proceeds, is essentially perpetual, and is always converted, and indissoluble according to order.

Proposition 35.

Every thing caused, abides in, proceeds from, and returns, or is converted to, its cause.

For if it alone abided, it would in no respect differ from its cause, being without separation and distinction from it. For progression in accompanied with separation. But if it alone proceeded, it would be unconjoined and deprived of sympathy with its cause, having no communication with it whatever. And if it were alone converted, how can that which has not its essence from the cause, be essentially converted to that which is foreign to its nature? But if it should abide and proceed, but should not be converted, how will there be a natural desire to every thing of well-being, and of good, and an excitation to its generating cause? And if it should proceed and be converted, but should not abide, how being separated from its cause will it hasten to be conjoined with it? For it was unconjoined prior to its departure; since if it had been conjoined, it would entirely have abided in it. But if it should abide and be converted, but should not proceed, how can that which is not[24] separated be able to revert to its cause? For every thing which is converted resembles that which is resolved into the nature from which it is essentially divided. It is necessary however, either that it should abide alone, or be converted alone, or alone proceed, or that the extremes should be bound to each other, or that the medium should be conjoined with each of the extremes, or that all should be conjoined. Hence it remains that every thing must abide in its cause, proceed from, and be converted to it.

Proposition 36.

Of all things which are multiplied according to progression, the first are more perfect than the second, the second than those posterior to them, and after the same manner successively.

For if progressions separate productions from their causes, and there are diminutions of things secondary with respect to such as are first, it follows that first natures in proceeding, are more conjoined with their causes, being [as it were,] germinations from them. But second natures are more remote from their causes, and in a similar manner such as are successive. Things however, which are nearer and more allied to their causes, are more perfect. For causes are more perfect than things caused. But things which are more remote are more imperfect, being dissimilar to their causes.

Proposition 37.

Of all things which subsist according to conversion, the first are more imperfect than the second, and the second than those that follow; but the last are the most perfect.

For if conversions are effected in a circle, and conversion is directed to that from which progression is derived, but progression is from that which is most perfect, hence conversion is directed to the most perfect. And if conversion first begins from that in which progression terminates, but progression terminates in that which is most imperfect, conversion will begin from the most imperfect. Hence in things which subsist according to conversion, such as are most imperfect are the first, but such as are most perfect, the last.

Proposition 38.

Every thing which proceeds from certain numerous causes, is converted through as many causes as those are through which it proceeds, and all conversion is through the same things as those through which progression is effected.

For since each of these takes place through similitude, that indeed which has a transition immediately from a certain thing, is also immediately converted to it. For the similitude here is without a medium. But that which requires a medium in proceeding, requires also a medium according to conversion. For it is necessary that each should be effected with reference to the same thing. Hence the conversion will be first to the medium, and afterwards to that which is better than the medium. Through such things therefore as being is derived to each thing, through so many well-being also is derived, and vice versa.

Proposition 39.

Every being is either alone essentially converted, or vitally, or also gnostically.

For either it alone possesses being from its cause, or life together with being, or it likewise receives from thence a gnostic power. So far therefore as it alone *is*, it makes an essential conversion, but so far as it lives, a vital, and so far as it likewise knows, a gnostic conversion. For in such a way as it proceeded from its cause, such also is the mode of its conversion to it, and the measures of its conversion are defined by the measures according to progression. Desire therefore is to some things according to being alone, this desire being an aptitude to the participation of causes; but to others it is according to life, being a motion to more excellent natures; and to others, it is according to knowledge, being a co-sensation of the goodness of causes.

Proposition 40.

Of all things which proceed from another cause, those which exist from themselves, and which are allotted a self-subsistent essence, are the leaders.

For if every thing which is sufficient to itself, either according to essence, or according to energy, is more excellent than that which is suspended from another cause; but that which produces itself, since it produces the being of itself, is sufficient to itself with respect to essence; but that which is alone produced by another is not sufficient to itself; and the self-sufficient is more allied to *the good;* but things more allied and similar to their causes, subsist from cause prior to such as are dissimilar;—this being the case, things which are produced by themselves, and are self-subsistent, are more ancient than those which proceed into existence from another cause alone. For either there will be nothing self-subsistent, or *the good* is a thing of this kind, or the first things that subsist from *the good.* But if there is nothing self-subsistent, there will not in reality be in any thing self-sufficiency. Nor will it be in *the good,* since that being *the one* is better than self-sufficiency. It is also *the good itself,* and not that which possesses *the good*. But if *the good* was self-subsistent, in consequence of itself producing itself, it will not be *the one*. For that which proceeds from *the one* is not *the one*. And it would proceed from itself, if it was self-subsistent; so that *the* one, would at the same time be one and not one. Hence, it is necessary that the self-subsistent should be posterior to the first. And it is evident that it will be prior to things which alone proceed from another cause. For it has a more principal subsistence than these, and is more allied to *the good*, as has been demonstrated.

Proposition 41.

Every thing which is in another is alone produced by another; but every thing which is in itself is self-subsistent.

For that which is in another thing and is indigent of a subject, can never be generative of itself. For that which is naturally adapted to generate itself, does not require another seat, because it is contained by itself, and is preserved in itself apart from a subject. But that which abides, and is able to be established in itself, is productive of itself, itself proceeding into itself, and being connective of itself. And thus it is in itself, as the thing caused in its cause. For it is not in itself, as in place, or as in a subject. For place is different from that which is in place, and that which is in a subject is different from the subject. But this which is in itself is the same with that in which it is inherent; for it is self-subsistent. And it is in such a manner in itself, as that which is from a cause is in the cause.

Proposition 42.

Every thing self-subsistent is convertive to itself.

For if it proceeds from itself, it will also make a conversion to itself. For to that from which progression is derived, to that a conversion coordinate to the progression is directed. For if it alone proceeded from itself, but having proceeded was not converted to itself, it would never aspire after its proper good, and that which it is able to impart to itself. Every cause however is able to impart to that which proceeds from it,[25] together with the essence which it gives, well-being conjoined with this essence. Hence that which is self-subsistent will impart this to itself. This therefore is the proper good to that which is self-subsistent. And hence this will not be the object of desire to that which is not[26] converted to itself. But not desiring this, it will not obtain it, and not obtaining it, it will be imperfect, and not sufficient to itself. If, however, self-sufficiency and perfection pertain to any thing, they must pertain to that which is self-subsistent. Hence it will obtain its proper good, and will be converted to itself.

Proposition 43.

Every thing which is convertive to itself is self-subsistent.

For if it is converted to itself according to nature, it is perfect in the conversion to itself, and will possess essence from itself. For to every thing, essential progression is from that to which conversion according to nature is directed. If therefore, it imparts well-being to itself, it will likewise undoubtedly impart being to itself, and will be the lord of it own hypostasis. Hence, that which is able to revert to itself is self-subsistent.

Proposition 44.

Every thing which it convertive to itself according to energy, is also converted to itself essentially.

For if it is capable of being converted to itself in energy, but is without conversion in its essence, it will be more excellent according to energy than according to essence, the former being convertive, but the latter without conversion. For that which depends on itself, is better than that which alone depends on another. And that which has a power of preserving itself, is more perfect than that which is alone preserved by another. If therefore, it is convertive to itself according to the energy proceeding from essence,[27] it will also be allotted a convertive essence, so that it will not alone energize towards itself, but will depend on itself, and will be contained, connected, and perfected by itself.

Proposition 45.

Every thing self-subsistent is unbegotten.

For if it is generated, because generated indeed, it will be imperfect of itself, and will be indigent of perfection from another. Because, however, it produces itself, it is perfect and sufficient to itself. For every thing generated is perfected by another which imparts generation to it not yet[28] existing. For generation is a path from the imperfect to its contrary the perfect. But if any thing produces itself, it is always perfect, being always present with the essence of itself, or rather being inherent in that which is perfective of essence.

Proposition 46.

Every thing self-subsistent is incorruptible.

For if it should be corrupted, it would desert itself, and would be without itself. This however is impossible. For being one thing, it is at the same time cause and the thing caused. But every thing which is corrupted, departing from the cause of itself is corrupted. For so far as it adheres to that which contains, connects and preserves it, it is connected and preserved. But that which is self-subsistent never leaves its cause, because it does not desert itself; for it is the cause of itself. Every thing therefore self-subsistent is incorruptible.

Proposition 47.

Every thing self-subsistent, is impartible and simple.

For if it is partible, being self-subsistent, it will constitute itself partible,[29] and the whole will be converted to itself, and all will be in all itself. This however is impossible. Hence that which is self-subsistent is impartible. But it is also simple. For if a composite, one thing in it will be less, but another more excellent, and the more will be derived from the less excellent, and the less from the more excellent, if the whole proceeds from itself. Farther still, it would not be sufficient to itself, being indigent of the elements of itself of which it consists. Every thing therefore, which is self-subsistent, is simple.

Proposition 48.

Concerning the perpetual, in order to demonstrate that the world is perpetual.

Every thing which is not perpetual, is either a composite, or subsists in another.

For either it is dissoluble into those things of which it consists, and is entirely composed from the things into which it is dissolved, or it is indigent of a subject, and leaving the subject it departs into non-entity. But if it is simple in itself, it will be indissoluble, and incapable of being dissipated.

Proposition 49.

Every thing self-subsistent is perpetual.

For there are two modes according to which it is necessary a thing should not be perpetual; the one arising from composition, and the other from a subsistence in something else [as in a subject]. That which is self-subsistent however, is neither a composite, but simple, nor in another, but in itself. Hence it is perpetual.

Proposition 50.

Every thing which is measured by time, either according to essence, or according to energy, is generation, so far as it is measured by time.

For if it is measured by time, it will be adapted to it to be, or to energize in time; and the *was* and the *will be,* which differ from each other, pertain to it. For if the *was* and the *will be* were the same according to number, it would suffer nothing by time proceeding, and always having one part prior, and another posterior. If therefore the *was* and the *will be* are different, that which is measured by time is becoming to be [or rising into existence], and never *is,*[30] but proceeds together with time, by which it is measured, existing in a tendency to being.

It likewise does not stop in the same state of being, but is always receiving another and another *to be,* just as *the now* in time is always another and another, through the progression of time. Hence it is not a simultaneous whole; for it subsists in a dispersion of temporal extension, and is co-extended with time. This however is to possess being in non-being. For that which is becoming to be is not that which is become. Such a kind of being therefore as this is generation.

Proposition 51.

Every thing self-subsistent, is essentially exempt from the natures which are measured by time.

For if that which is self-subsistent is unbegotten, it will not according to existence be measured by time. For generation is conversant with the nature which is measured by time. Hence nothing self-subsistent has its being in time.

Proposition 52.

Every thing eternal is a whole which subsists at once. And whether it has its essence alone eternal, it will possess the whole at once present, nor will it have *this* thing pertaining to itself now subsisting, but *that* afterwards which as yet is not; but as much as is possible it now possesses the whole without diminution, and without extension. Or whether it has its energy as well as its essence at once present, it possesses this also collectively, abiding in the same measure of perfection, and as it were, fixed immovably and without transition according to one and the same boundary.

For if the eternal, as the name denotes, is perpetual being, but to be sometimes,[1] and to subsist in becoming to be, are different from perpetual being, it is not proper that it should have one thing prior and another posterior. For if it had, it would be generation, and not being. But where there is neither prior nor posterior, nor was and will be, but alone *to be,* and this a whole, there every thing subsists at once that which it is. The same thing also takes place with respect to the energy of that which is eternal.

Corollary.

From this it is evident that eternity is the cause to wholes of their existence as wholes, since every thing which is eternal either according to essence, or according to energy, has the whole of its essence or energy present with itself.

Proposition 53.

Concerning Eternity and Eternal Natures.

Eternity subsists prior to all eternal natures, and time exists prior to every thing which subsists according to time.

For if every where the natures which are participated are prior to their participants, and imparticipables are prior to participated natures, it is evident that the eternal is one thing, the eternity which is in the eternal, another, and eternity itself, another. And the first of these indeed subsists as a participant, the second as a thing participated, and the third as an imparticipable. That also which is in time is one thing; for it is a participant. The time which is in this is another thing; for it is participated. And the time prior to this is another thing; for it is imparticipable. Every where also, that which is imparticipable is in all things the same. But that which is participated is in those things only by which it is participated. For there are many eternal, and many temporal natures in all of which eternity subsists according to participation. The time also which is in temporal natures subsists in a distributed manner; but the time which they participate is indivisible. And there is one time prior to both these. Eternity itself likewise is an eternity of eternities, and time itself is a time of times; and they give subsistence, the one to participated eternity, but the other to participated time.

Proposition 54.

Every eternity is the measure of eternal natures, and every time is the measure of things in time; and these are the only two measures of life and motion in beings.

For every thing which measures, either measures according to a part, or it measures the whole at once when it is adapted to that which is measured. That which measures, therefore, according to the whole is eternity; but that which measures according to parts is time. Hence, there are only two measures, the one of things eternal, but the other of things in time.

Proposition 55.

Every thing which subsists according to time, either subsists through the whole of time, or has its hypostasis once in a part of time.

For if all progressions are through similitude, and things more similar to first natures subsist in union with them prior to such as are dissimilar, but it is impossible for things which are generated in a part of time to be conjoined with eternal natures, (for as being generated they differ from first natures which are self-subsistent,[32] and as existing once, they are separated from things which always exist, but the media between these, are such things as are partly similar and partly dissimilar to them)—this being the case, the medium between things which are once generated, and those that exist always, is either that which is always becoming to be, or that which is once, or that which is not truly being. It is however impossible it should be that which once only truly is. And that which is once not truly being is the same with that which is becoming to be. Hence the medium is not that which is once only. It remains, therefore, that the medium between both is that which is always becoming to be, being conjoined indeed with the worse of the two through becoming to be, but through subsisting always, imitating an eternal nature.

Corollary.

From these things it is evident that perpetuity is twofold, the one indeed being eternal, but the other subsisting according to time. The one also being a stable, but the other a flowing perpetuity. And the one indeed having its being collected, and the whole subsisting at once, bat the other diffused, and expanded according to temporal extension. And the one being a whole of itself, but the other consisting of parts, each of which is separate, according to prior and posterior.

Proposition 56.

Every thing which is produced by secondary natures, is produced in a greater degree by prior and more causal natures, by whom such as are secondary were also produced.

For if that which is secondary has the whole of its essence from that which is prior to it, its power of producing is also derived from thence; for powers in producing causes are essentially productive, and give completion to the essence of them. But if it is allotted the power of producing from a superior cause, it will possess from that its existence as the cause of things of which it is the cause, and its power of giving subsistence to other things will be measured from thence. If, however, this be the case, the things proceeding from it are effects through that which is prior to it. For the one perfects a cause, and the other the thing caused. But if this be the case, the thing caused is from thence rendered such as it is.

Moreover, that it is also in a greater degree perfected from thence is evident. For if that which is first gives to that which is second the cause of producing, it will primarily possess this cause; and on this account that which is secondary generates, receiving from thence a secondary generative power. If, however, the one becomes productive through participation, but the other in a way superior to participation and primarily, that will be in a greater degree a cause, which imparts generative power to another thing proximate to its own nature.

Proposition 57.

Every cause both energizes prior to the thing caused, and gives subsistence to a greater number of effects posterior to it.

For so far as it is cause, it is more perfect and more powerful than that which is posterior to it, and in consequence of this is the cause of a greater number of effects. For it is the province of a greater power to produce more, of an equal power to produce equal, and of a less power to produce a less number of effects. And the power which is able to effect greater things among similars, is also capable of effecting such as are less. But that which is able to effect such as are less, is not necessarily capable of producing such as are greater. If, therefore, the cause is more powerful, it is productive of more numerous effects.

Moreover, such effects as the thing caused is able to produce, the cause is in a greater degree able to produce. For every thing which is produced by secondary natures, is in a greater degree produced by such as are prior and more causal. The cause, therefore, gives subsistence together with the thing caused to such effects as the thing caused is naturally adapted to produce. But if likewise it produces prior to it, it is indeed evident that it energizes prior to the thing caused, according to the energy which is productive of it. Every cause, therefore, energies prior to the thing caused, and together with it, and posterior to it, gives subsistence to other things.

Corollary.

Hence, it is evident, that of such things as soul is the cause, intellect also is the cause; but that soul is not also the cause of such things as intellect is the cause. But intellect energizes prior to soul. And such things as soul imparts to secondary natures, intellect also imparts in a greater degree. Likewise, when soul no longer energizes, intellect imparts by illumination the gifts of itself to those things to which soul does not impart herself. For that which is inanimate, so far as it participates of form, participates of intellect, and the production of intellect. Moreover, of such things as intellect is the cause, *the good* also is the cause; but not vice versa. For the privations of forms subsist from *the good;* since all things are from thence. But intellect being form, does not give subsistence to privation.

Proposition 58.

Every thing which is produced by many, is more compounded than that which is produced by fewer causes.

For if every cause imparts something to that which proceeds from it, more numerous causes will impart a greater number of gifts, but less numerous causes a less number. Hence, of participants some will consist of a greater number of things, but others, of a less number, of which each participates, some indeed through a progression from a greater number of causes, but others from a less. Those, however, which proceed from a greater number of causes are more compounded, but those from a less number of the same causes, are more simple. Every thing, therefore, which is produced by a greater number of causes, is more compounded, but that which is produced by a less number is more simple. For the more compounded participates of those things of which the more simple participates, but the contrary to this is not true.

Proposition 59.

Every thing which is essentially simple, is either better or worse than composite natures

For if such beings as are the extremes of things are produced by fewer and more simple causes, but such as are in the middle, from a greater number of causes, the latter indeed will be composites, but of the former, some are more simple according to that which is better, but others according to that which is worse. That the extremes, however, are produced by fewer causes is evident, because such natures as are higher begin to produce prior to such as are subordinate, and extend beyond them, to things to which subordinate natures do not proceed through a diminution of power. For on this account also, the last of things, [*i.e.* matter] is most simple, as well as the first of things, because it proceeds from the first alone. With respect to simplicity, however, one kind subsists according to that which is better than all composition, but another according to that which is worse. And there is the same reasoning in all things.

Proposition 60.

Every thing which is the cause of a greater number of effects, is better than that which is allotted a power of producing a less number, and which produces the parts of those things to the wholes of which the other gives subsistence.

For if the one is the cause of a less, hut the other of a greater number of effects, but the former are parts of the latter, that which gives subsistence to a greater number of effects, will produce all that the other produces; but not vice versa. Hence the former of these two is more powerful and more comprehensive. For as that which proceeds is to that which proceeds, so is one productive power to another, when assumed with reference to each other. For that which is able to effect a greater number of things, possesses a greater and more total power. But this is nearer to the cause of all things. That however, which is nearer to this cause, is in a greater degree good, just as the cause of all is *the good* itself. Hence, that which is the cause of a greater number of effects, is essentially more excellent than that which produces a less number.

Proposition 61.

Every power which is impartible is greater, but when divided is less.

For if it is divided it proceeds into multitude. And if this be the case, it becomes more remote from *the one*. But in consequence of this it is able to effect a less number of things, through departing, from *the one*, and the unity which contains it, and will be imperfect, since the good of every thing consists in union.

Proposition 62.

Every multitude which is nearer to *the one,* is less in quantity than things more remote from it, but is greater in power.

For that which is nearer to is more similar to *the one*. But *the one* gives subsistence to all things, without having any multitude in itself. Hence that which is more similar to it, being the cause of a greater number of effects, since *the one* is the cause of all things, has more the form of unity, and is more impartible, because that is *one*. As, therefore, that which is less multiplied, is more allied to *the one,* so likewise as being allied to the cause of all things, it is productive of a greater number of effects. Hence it is more powerful.

Corollary.

From these things it is evident, that there are more corporeal natures than souls; more souls than intellectual natures; and more intellects than divine unities. And there is the same reasoning in all things.

Proposition 63.

Every thing which is imparticipable gives subsistence to two-fold orders of participated natures, one indeed in things which sometimes participate, but the other in things which always and connascently participate.

For that which is always participated, is more similar to the imparticipable than that which is sometimes participated. Hence, before the imparticipable establishes that which is sometimes, it will establish that which is always participable; and which by being participated differs from that which is posterior to it, but by *the always* is more allied and more similar to the imparticipable. Nor are there alone things which are sometimes participated; for prior to these are the natures which are always participated, through which these also are bound to imparticipables according to a certain well ordered progression. Nor are there alone things which are sometimes participated. For these possessing an inextinguishable power, since they are always, are prolific of other things which are sometimes participated, and as far as to these the diminution proceeds

Corollary.

From hence it is evident that of the unions proceeding from *the one,* and which illuminate beings, some are always, but others sometimes participated. Intellectual participations, likewise, are in a similar manner two-fold, as also are the animations of souls, and the participations of other forms. For beauty, similitude, permanency, and sameness, being imparticipable, are participated by natures which always participate, and secondarily by those that sometimes participate according to the order.

Proposition 64.

Every monad which ranks as a principle, gives subsistence to a two-fold number; one indeed of self-perfect hypostases, but the other of illuminations which possess their hypostasis in other things.

For if progression is according to diminution, through things appropriate to producing causes, perfect natures will proceed from the all-perfect, and through these as media, imperfect natures will proceed in a well-ordered progression, so that some indeed will be self-perfect hypostases, but others will be imperfect. And these latter will become the forms of participants. For being imperfect, they will be indigent of subjects in their very nature. But the self-perfect hypostases will produce things which participate of themselves. For being perfect, they will indeed fill these from themselves, and establish them in themselves. But they will require nothing of inferior natures to their own subsistence. Self-perfect hypostases, therefore, through their separation into multitude, are indeed diminished with respect to their principal monad; but through their self-perfect hyparxis, they are in a certain respect assimilated to it. But imperfect hypostases, in consequence of subsisting in other things, are remote from that which subsists from itself, and through their imperfection are separated from that which perfects all things. Progressions, however, are through similars, as far as to natures which are entirely dissimilar. Every monad, therefore, which ranks as a principle, gives subsistence to a two-fold number.

Corollary.

From these things it is evident, that of the unities, some are self-perfect proceeding from *the one,* but others are illuminations of unions. And with respect to intellects, that some of them are self-perfect essences, but others belong to animated natures, being only the images of souls. And thus, neither is every union a God, but this is true of a self-perfect unity alone, nor is every intellectual peculiarity an intellect, but an essential peculiarity alone [is entitled to this appellation], nor is every illumination of soul a soul, but there are also images of souls.

Proposition 65.

Every thing which has any subsistence whatever, either subsists according to cause, so as to have the form of a principle, or according to hyparxis, or according to participation, after the manner of an image.

For either that which is produced is seen in that which produces, as pre-existing in cause, because every cause antecedently comprehends in itself the thing caused, being that primarily which the thing caused is secondarily. Or that which produces is seen in that which is produced. For the latter participating of the former, exhibits in itself secondarily that which the producing cause is primarily. Or each thing is beheld in its own order, and is neither seen in the cause nor in the effect. For the cause subsists more excellently than that which exists [out of the cause]. But that which is in the effect is less excellent than that which exists out of the cause [but is not in any thing else]. It is, however, necessary there should be that which after this manner *is.* But every thing subsists according to hyparxis in its own order.

Proposition 66.

All beings with reference to each other, are either wholes, or parts, or the same, or different.

For either some of them comprehend, but the rest are comprehended, or they neither comprehend, nor are comprehended. And they either suffer something which is the same, as participating of one thing, or they are separated from each other. But if they comprehend, they will be wholes, and if they are comprehended, parts. If also many things participate of one thing, they are the same according to this one. But if they are alone many things, so far as they are many they will be different from each other.

Proposition 67.

Every wholeness (ολοτης) is either prior to parts, or consists of parts, or is in a part.

For the form of each thing is either surveyed in its cause, and we call that which subsists in its cause a whole prior to parts. Or it is seen in the parts which participate of it; and this in a two-fold respect. For it is either seen in all the parts together, and this is a whole consisting of parts, any part of which being absent diminishes the whole. Or it is seen in each of the parts, so that the part also becomes according to participation a whole; which makes the part to be a whole partially. The whole, therefore, which is according to hyparxis consists of parts. But the whole which is prior to parts is according to cause. And the whole which is in a part is according to participation. For this also according to an ultimate diminution is a whole, so far as it imitates the whole which consists of parts, when it is not any casual part, but is capable of being assimilated to the whole, of which the parts also are wholes.

Proposition 68.

Every whole which is in a part, is a part of that whole which consists of parts.

For if it is a part, it is a part of a certain whole. And it is either a part of the whole which it contains, according to which it is said to be a whole in a part. But thus it will be a part of itself, the part will be equal to the whole, and each will be the same. Or it is a part of a certain other whole. And if of some other, it is either the only part of that, and thus again, it will in no respect differ from the whole, being one part of one thing. Or it is a part in conjunction with another part. For of every whole the parts are more than one, and that will be a whole from many parts, of which it consists. And thus the whole which is in a part, is a part of the whole which consists of parts.

Proposition 69.

Every whole which consists of parts, participates of the wholeness which is prior to parts

For if it consists of parts, the whole is passive [*i.e.* the whole participates of another whole]. For the parts becoming one, are passive to a whole on account of their union, and the whole subsists in parts which are not wholes. But the imparticipable subsists prior to every thing which is participated. The imparticipable wholeness, therefore, subsists prior to that which is participated. Hence, there is a certain form of wholeness, prior to the whole which consists of parts, which is not passive to a whole, but is wholeness itself, and from which the wholeness consisting of parts is derived. For the whole indeed, which consists of parts, subsists in many places, and in many things, in various ways. It is, however, necessary that there should be a monad essentially of all totalities. For neither is each of these wholes genuine, since it is indigent of parts that are not wholes, of which it consists. Nor is the whole which is in a certain thing capable of being the cause of wholeness to all other things. Hence, that which is the cause to all wholes of their being wholes, is prior to parts. For if this also consisted of parts, it would be a certain whole, and not simply whole. And again, this would be from another whole, and so on, to infinity; or it will subsist on account of that which is primarily a whole, and which is not a whole from parts, but is a wholeness.

Proposition 70.

Every thing which is more total among principal causes, illuminates participants, prior to partial natures, and when these fail, still continues to impart its illuminations.

For it begins its energy upon secondary natures prior to that which is posterior to it, and is present in conjunction with the presence of it. When likewise that which is posterior to it no longer energizes, it is still present, and that which is more causal continues to energize. And this not only in different subjects, but likewise in each of the natures that sometimes participate. Thus it is necessary, for instance, that being should be first generated, afterwards animal, and afterwards man. And man, indeed, is not, if the rational power is absent, but there is still animal, breathing and sentient. And again, life failing, being remains. For though a thing does not live, yet it has existence. And there is a similar reasoning in all things.

The cause, however, of this is, that the more causal nature being more efficacious, energizes on the thing caused[33] prior [to that which is less causal]. For the thing caused participates first of that which is more powerful. And that which is secondary again energizing, that which is more powerful energizes with it. Because every thing which the secondary nature produces, that which is more causal produces likewise in conjunction with it. When the former also fails, the latter is still present. For the communication of the more powerful cause, operating in a greater degree, leaves that which participates it, posterior to the energy of the less powerful cause. For through the communication of the secondary nature, it corroborates its own illumination.

Proposition 71.

All things which among principal causes possess a more total and higher order in their effects, according to the illuminations proceeding from them, become in a certain respect subjects to the communications of more partial causes. And the illuminations indeed, from higher causes, receive the progressions from secondary causes; but the latter are established in the former. And thus some participations precede others, and some representations extend after others, beginning from on high, to the same subject, more total causes having a prior energy, but such as are more partial, supplying their participants with their communications, posterior to the energies of more total causes.

For if more causal natures energize prior to such as are secondary on account of exuberance of power, and are present with those that have a more imperfect aptitude, and illuminate them also; but things more subordinate, and which are second in order, are supplied from such as are more causal,—it is evident that the illuminations of superior natures antecedently comprehend that which participates of both these, and give stability to the communications of things subordinate. But these illuminations of superior causes, employ the resemblances of subordinate natures as foundations, and operate on that which participates of them, the superior causes themselves having a prior energy.

Proposition 72.

All things which in their participants have the relation of a subject, proceed from more perfect and total causes.

For the causes of a greater number of effects, are more powerful and total, and are nearer to *the one* than the causes of fewer effects. But the natures which give subsistence to such things as are antecedently the subjects of others, are among causes the sources of a greater number of effects.

Corollary.

From hence it is evident why matter which derives its subsistence from *the one,* is of itself destitute of form. And why body, though it participates of being, is of itself without the participation of soul. For matter being the subject of all things proceeds from the cause of all. But body being the subject of animation, derives its subsistence from that which is more total than soul, and participates after a certain manner of being.

Proposition 73.

Every whole is at the same time a certain being, and participates of being, but not every being is a whole.[34]

For either being and whole are the same, or the one is prior, but the other posterior. If, however, a part, so far as it is a part, is being (for a whole is from parts which have a being), yet it is not of itself also a whole. Being, therefore, and whole are not the same. For if this were the case, a part would be a non-entity. But if a part was a non-entity, the whole would have no existence. For every whole is a whole of parts, either as existing prior to them [and therefore causally containing them in itself], or as subsisting in them. But the part not existing, neither is it possible for the whole to exist. If, however, whole is prior to being, every being will immediately be a whole. Again, therefore, there will not be a part. This, however, is impossible. For if the whole is a whole, being the whole of a part, the part also being a part, will be the part of the whole. It remains, therefore, that every whole indeed is being, but that not every being is a whole.

Corollary.

From these things, it is evident that being which has a primary subsistence is beyond wholeness. For the one indeed, *viz.* being, is present with a greater number of things; since *to be* is present with parts, so far as they *are* parts. But the other, *viz.* wholeness, is present with a less number of things. For that which is the cause of a greater number of effects is more excellent; but the cause of a less number is of a subordinate nature, as has been demonstrated.

Proposition 74.

Every form is a certain whole; for it consists of many things, each of which gives completion to the form. But not every whole is a form.

For a particular[35] thing is a whole and also an individual, so far it is an individual, but neither of them is a form. For every whole consists of parts; but form is that which may be divided into individual forms. Whole, therefore, is one thing, and form another. And the one is present with many things, but the other with a few. Hence, whole is above the forms of beings.

Corollary.

From these things it is evident that whole has a middle order between being and forms. And hence it follows that being subsists prior to forms, and that forms are beings, but that not every being is form. Whence also, in effects, privations are in a certain respect beings, but are no longer forms, and in consequence of the unical power of being, they also receive a certain obscure representation of being.[36]

Proposition 75.

Every cause which is properly so called, is exempt from its effect.

For if it is in the effect, it either gives completion to it, or is in a certain respect indigent of it in order to its existence; and thus it will be more imperfect than the thing caused. For being in the effect, it is rather a concause than a cause, and is either a part of that which is generated, of an instrument of the maker. For that which is a part in the thing generated, is more imperfect than the whole. The cause also which is is the effect, is an instrument of generation to the maker, being unable to define of itself the measures of production. Every cause, therefore, which is properly so denominated, if it is more perfect than that which proceeds from it, imparts to its effect the measure of generation, and is exempt from instruments and elements, and in short, from every thing which is called a concause.

Proposition 76.

Every thing which is generated from an immoveable cause, has as immutable hyparxis. But every thing which is generated from a moveable cause, has a mutable hyparxis.

For if that which makes is entirely immoveable, it does not produce from itself that which is secondary through motion, but by its very being. If, however, this be the case, it has that which proceeds from it concurrent with its own essence. And if this also be the case, it will produce as long as it exists. But it exists always, and therefore it always gives subsistence to that which is posterior to itself. Hence, this is always generated from thence, and always is, conjoining with *the ever* according to energy of the cause, its own ever according to progression. If, however, the cause is moved, that also which is generated from it will be essentially mutable. For that which has its being through motion, changes its being when its moveable cause[37] is changed. For if, though produced from motion, it should itself remain immutable, it would be better than its producing cause. This, however, is impossible. It will not, therefore, be immutable. Hence, it will be mutable, and will be essentially moved, imitating the motion of that which gave it subsistence.

Proposition 77.

Every thing which is in capacity proceeds from that which is in energy. And that which is in capacity, proceeds into energy. That also which is in a certain respect in capacity, so far as it is in capacity, is the offspring of that which is in a certain respect in energy. But that which is all things in capacity, proceeds from that which is all things in energy.

For that which is in capacity is not naturally adapted to produce itself into energy, because it is imperfect. For if being imperfect it should become the cause to itself of perfection, and this in energy, the cause will be more imperfect than that which is produced by it. Hence, that which is in capacity, so far as it is in capacity, will not be the cause to itself of a subsistence in energy. For on this hypothesis, so far as it is imperfect, it would be the cause of perfection; since every thing which is in capacity, so far as it is in capacity, is imperfect, but that which is in energy is perfect. Hence, if that which was in capacity becomes in energy, it will have its perfection from something else. And this will either be in capacity; but thus again the imperfect will be generative of the perfect; or it will be in energy, and either something else, or this which was in capacity will be that which becomes in energy. But if something else which is in energy produces, operating according to its own peculiarity, it will not by being in capacity make that which is in another to be energy; nor will this which is now made be in energy, unless it becomes this so far as it was in capacity. It remains, therefore, that from that which is in energy, that which is in capacity must be changed into energy.

Proposition 78.

Every power is either perfect or imperfect.

For the power which is prolific of energy is perfect. For it makes other things to be perfect through its own energies. That, however, which is perfective of other things is in a greater degree perfect, as being more self-perfect . But the power which is indigent of another that pre-exists in energy, according to which indigence it is something in capacity, is imperfect. For it is indigent of the perfection which is in another, in order that by participating of it, it may become perfect. Hence, such a power as this is of itself imperfect. So that the power of that which is in energy is perfect, being prolific of energy. But the power of that which is in capacity is imperfect, and obtains perfection from the power which is in energy.

Proposition 79.

Every thing which is generated, is generated from a two-fold power.[38]

For it is requisite that the thing generated should possess aptitude and an imperfect power. And that which makes being in energy[39] that which the thing generated is in capacity, antecedently comprehends a perfect power. For all energy proceeds from inherent power. For if that which makes did not possess power, how could it energize, and produce something else? And if that which is generated did not possess power according to aptitude, how could it be generated? For that which makes or acts, makes or acts in that which is able to suffer, but not in any casual thing, and which is not naturally adapted to suffer from the agent.

Proposition 80.

Every body is naturally adapted of itself to suffer; but every thing incorporeal to act. And the former indeed is essentially inefficacious, but the latter is impassive. That which is incorporeal, however, suffers through its communion with body; just as bodies are able to act through the participation of incorporeals.

For body, so far as body, is alone divisible, and through this becomes passive, being entirely partible, and this to infinity. But that which is incorporeal, being simple, is impassive. For neither is that which is impartible, capable of being divided, nor can that be changed in quality which is not compounded. Either, therefore, nothing will be effective, or this must be affirmed of an incorporeal nature, since body, so far as body, does not act, because it is alone liable to be divided, and to suffer. For every thing which acts has an effective power; so that body, so far as it is body, will not act, but so far as it contains in itself a power of acting. Hence, when it acts, it acts through the participation of power. Moreover, incorporeal natures when they are inherent in bodies, participate of passions, being divided together with bodies, and enjoying their partible nature, though according to their own essence they are impartible.

Proposition 81.

Every thing which is participated in a separable manner, is present with its participant by a certain inseparable power which it inserts in it.

For if it is itself present with the participant in a separate manner, and is not in it, as if it possessed its subsistence in it, a certain medium between the two is necessary, connecting the one with the other, and which is more similar to that which is participated, and subsists in the participant. For if this medium is separable, how can it be participated by the participant, since the participant neither contains the medium, nor any thing proceeding from it? A power, therefore, and illumination proceeding from that which is separable into the participant conjoins both. Hence, one of these will be that through which the participation is effected, another will be that which is participated, and another that which participates.

Proposition 82.

Every thing incorporeal, which is converted to itself, when it is participated by other things, is participated in a separable manner.

For if in an inseparable manner, the energy of it would not be separate from its participant, as neither would its essence. If, however, this were the case, it would not be converted to itself. For being converted, it will be separate from its participant, each being different from the other. If, therefore, it is able to be converted to itself, it will be participated in a separable manner, when it is participated by other things.

Proposition 83.

Every thing which has a knowledge of itself, is entirely converted to itself.

For knowing itself, it is evident that it is converted to itself in energy. For that which knows and that which is known are one. And the knowledge of itself is directed to itself as to that which is known. This knowledge also as pertaining to that which knows is a certain energy; but it is the knowledge of itself directed to itself, because it is gnostic of itself. Moreover, that it is converted to itself essentially, if it is so in energy, has been demonstrated. For every thing which by energizing is converted to itself, has also an essence verging to, and subsisting in itself.

Proposition 84.

Every thing which always is, possesses an infinite power.

For if its hypostasis is never-failing, the power also according to which it is that which it is, and is able to exist, is infinite. For the power of existing being finite, it will some time or other fail. But this failing, the existence also of that which possesses it will fail, and it will no longer be that which always is. It is necessary, therefore, that the power of that which always is, and which connects and contains it essentially, should be infinite.

Proposition 85.

Every thing which is always becoming to be, or rising into existence, (αει γινομενον) possesses an infinite power of becoming to be.

For if it is always rising into existence, the power of generation in it is never-failing. For if this power was finite, it would cease in an infinite time. But the power of becoming to be ceasing, that which is rising into being according to this power would cease, and thus it would no longer be always becoming to be.[40] It is, however, supposed to be always becoming to be. Hence, it possesses an infinite power of rising into existence.

Proposition 86.

Every thing which is truly being (οντως ον) is infinite, neither according to multitude, nor according to magnitude, but according to power alone.

For every infinite, is either in discrete, or in continued quantity, or in power. But that which always is, is infinite, as having an inextinguishable life, a never-failing hyparxis, and an undiminished energy. That which is eternally being, however, is neither infinite on account of magnitude; for that which is truly being is without magnitude, being self-subsistent; since every thing self-subsistent is impartible and simple. Nor is it infinite on account of multitude; for it has in the most eminent degree the form of *the one,* as being arranged most near, and being most allied to it. But it is infinite according to power. Hence, it is also impartible and infinite. And by how much the more it is one and impartible, by so much the more is it infinite. For the power which is divided, becomes imbecil and finite, and powers which are entirely divided, are in every respect finite. For ultimate powers, and which are most remote from *the one,* are in a certain respect finite, on account of their distribution into parts. But first powers, on account of their impartibility, are infinite. For a separation into parts divulses and dissolves the power of every thing. But impartibility compressing and contracting that which it contains, renders it never-failing, and undiminished in itself.

Moreover, infinity, according to magnitude, and also according to multitude, is entirely a privation and falling off from impartibility. For that which is finite is most near to the impartible, but the infinite is most remote from it, entirely departing from *the one.* Hence, that which is infinite according to power, is not infinite either according to multitude or magnitude, since infinite power subsists in conjunction with impartibility. But the infinite either in multitude or magnitude, is most remote from the impartible. If, therefore, that which is truly being was infinite either in magnitude or multitude, it would not possess infinite power. It does, however, possess infinite power; and therefore is not infinite either according to multitude, or according to magnitude.

Proposition 87.

Every thing eternal indeed is being, but not every being is eternal.

For the participation of being is present in a certain respect with generated natures,[41] so far as each of these is not that which in no respect is. But if that which is generated is not entirely deprived of being, it is in a certain respect being. The eternal, however, is in no respect whatever present with generated natures, and especially not with such of these as do not even participate of the perpetuity which subsists according to the whole of time. Moreover, every thing eternal always is. For it participates of eternity, which imparts to the natures by which it is participated to be always that which they are. Being, therefore, is participated by a greater number of things than eternity. And hence being is beyond eternity. For by those natures by whom eternity is participated, being is also participated. But not every thing which participates of being, participates also of eternity.

Proposition 88.

Every thing[42] which is truly being, is either prior to eternity, or in eternity, or participates of eternity.

For that there is true being prior to eternity has been demonstrated. But true being is also in eternity. For eternity possesses the *always* in conjunction with *being*. And that which participates of eternity, has both the *always* and *being*, according to participation. Eternity, however, possesses the *always* primarily, but *being* according to participation. But being itself is primarily being.

Proposition 89.

Every thing which is primarily being consists of bound and infinity.

For if it possesses infinite power, it is evident that it is infinite, and on this account consists from the infinite. If also it is impartible, and has the form of *the one,* through this, it participates of bound. For that which participates of unity is bounded. Moreover, it is impartible, and therefore possesses infinite power. Hence every thing which is truly [or primarily] being consists of bound and infinity.

Proposition 90.

The first bound, and the first infinity subsist by themselves prior to every thing which consists of bound and the infinite.

For if beings which subsist by themselves, are prior to those which are *certain* beings, as being common to all essences, and principal causes, and not the causes of certain, but in short of all beings, it is necessary that the first bound, and the first infinity should be prior to that[43] which consists of both these. For the bound in that which is mixed [or the first being,] participates of infinity, and the infinite participates of bound. But of every thing, that which is the first, is nothing else than that which it is. It is not therefore proper that the first infinite should have the form of bound, or that the first bound should have the form of infinity. These therefore subsist primarily prior to that which is mixed.

Proposition 91.

Every power is either finite or infinite. But every finite power indeed derives its subsistence from infinite power. And infinite power subsists from the first infinity.

For the powers which have an existence at a certain time, are finite, falling from the infinity of existing always. But the powers of eternal beings are infinite, never deserting their own hyparxis.

Proposition 92.

Every multitude of infinite powers, is suspended from one first infinity, which does not subsist as a participated power, nor in things which are endued with power, but subsists by itself, not being the power of a certain participant, but the cause of all beings.

For though the first being possesses power, yet it is not power itself. For it has also bound. But the first power is infinity. For infinite powers are infinite, through the participation of infinity. Infinity itself therefore, will be prior to all powers, through which being also possesses infinite power, and all things participate of infinity. For infinity is not the first of things [or the ineffable principle of all] since that is the measure of all things, being *the good* and *the one*. Nor is infinity being. For this is infinite, but not infinity. Hence infinity subsists between that which is first and being, and is the cause of all infinite powers, and of all the infinity that is in beings.

Proposition 93.

Every infinite which is in [true] beings, is neither infinite to the natures that are above beings, nor is it infinite to itself.

For that by which each thing is infinite, by this also it exists uncircumscribed. But every thing which is in [true] beings, is bounded by itself, and by all the things prior to it. It remains therefore, that the infinite which is in [true] beings, is infinite to subordinate natures alone, above which it is so expanded in power, as to be incomprehensible by all of them. For in whatever manner they may extend themselves towards this infinite, yet it has something[44] entirely exempt from them. And though all things enter into it, yet it has something occult, and incomprehensible by secondary natures. Though likewise it evolves the powers which it contains, yet it possesses something on account of its union insurmountable, contracted, and surpassing the evolution of beings. Since however, it contains and bounds itself, it will not be infinite to itself, nor much less to the natures situated above it, since it has a portion of the infinity which is in them. For the powers of more total natures are more infinite, in consequence of being more total, and having an arrangement nearer to the first infinity.

Proposition 94.

Every perpetuity is indeed a certain infinity, but not every infinity is perpetuity.

For there are many infinites which have the infinite not on account of *the always,* such for instance, as the infinity according to magnitude, the infinity according to multitude, and the infinity of matter. And whatever else there may be of the like kind, which is infinite, either because it cannot be passed over, or through the indefiniteness of its essence. That perpetuity however is a certain infinity[45] is evident. For that which never fails is infinite. But this is that which always has its hypostasis inexhaustible. Infinity therefore, is prior to perpetuity. For that which gives subsistence to a greater number of effects, and is more total, is more causal. Hence, the first infinity is beyond eternity, and infinity itself is prior to eternity.

Proposition 95.

Every power which is more single, is more infinite than that which is multiplied.

For if of powers the first infinity is nearest to *the one*, that power which is more allied to *the one*, is in a greater degree infinite than that which recedes from it. For being multiplied it loses the form of *the one*, in which while it remained, it possessed a transcendency with respect to other powers, being connected and contained through its impartibility. For in partible natures themselves, the powers when congregated, are united,[46] but when divided, they are increased in number, and become obscured.

Proposition 96.

The power which is infinite of every finite body, is incorporeal.

For if it were corporeal, if this body indeed is finite,[47] the infinite will be contained in the finite. But if the body is infinite, it will not be power so far as it is body. For if so far as it is body it is finite, but power is infinite, it will not be power so far as it is body. Hence, the power which is infinite in a finite body is incorporeal.

Proposition 97.

In each series of things, every cause which has the relation of a leader, imparts to the whole series the peculiarity of itself; and that which the cause is primarily, the series is according to diminution.

For if it is the leader of the whole series, and all coordinate natures are co-arranged with reference to it, it is evident that it imparts to all that the series contains the one idea according to which they are arranged in that series. For either all things partake of similitude to this cause without a cause, or that which is the same in all is derived from it. But the former of these is impossible. For that which is without a cause is also fortuitous. But the fortuitous can never take place in things in which there is order, connection, and an invariable sameness of subsistence. From the cause therefore, which ranks as a leader, every series receives the peculiarity of the hypostasis of that cause. But if from it, it is evident that this is accompanied with a diminution and decrement adapted to secondary natures. For either the peculiarity exists similarly in the leader, and the natures that are secondary, and how in this case can the former be the leader, but the latter be allotted an hypostasis after the leader? Or it exists dissimilarly. And if this be the case, it is evident that sameness is derived to the multitude from one thing, but not vice versa. And the illustrious peculiarity of the series which is primarily in one thing [or the leader,] is secondarily in the multitude [suspended from the leading cause].

Proposition 98.

Every separate cause is at one and the same time every where and no where.

For by the communication of its own power it is every where. For this is a cause which replenishes the natures that are naturally adapted to participate of it, rules over all secondary beings, and is present to all things by the prolific progressions of its illuminations. But by an essence unmingled with things in place, and by its exempt purity, it is no where. For if it is separate, it is established above all things. In a similar manner also, it is in no one of the natures inferior to itself. For if it was alone every where, it would not indeed be prevented from being a cause, and from subsisting in all its participants. But it would not be prior to all of them in a separate manner. If also it was no where without being every where, it would not indeed be prevented from being prior to all things, and from being nothing pertaining to subordinate natures. But it would not be in all things, as causes are naturally adapted to be in their effects,[48] by the abundant and unenvying communications of themselves. In order therefore, that existing as a cause, it may be in all things that are able to partake of it, and that being separate in itself, it may be prior to all the natures that are filled by it, it is every where, and at the same time no where.

And it is not indeed partly every where and partly no where. For thus it would be divulsed and separate from itself, if one part of it was every where in all things, but another was no where, and prior to all things. But the whole of it is every where, and in a similar manner no where. For the things which are able to participate of it, meet with the whole of it, and find the whole present with themselves, that at the same time being wholly exempt from them. For the participant does not place this separate cause in itself, but participates of it as much as it is capable of receiving. Nor in the communication of itself does it become contracted by the multitude of the participations of it; for it is separate. Nor do its participants participate of it defectively; for that which imparts is every where.

Proposition 99.

Every imparticipable, so far as it is imparticipable, does not derive its subsistence from another cause. But it is itself the principle and cause of all its participants. And thus every principle in each series is unbegotten.

For if it is imparticipable in its own proper series, it is allotted the principality, and does not proceed from other things. For it would no longer be the first, if it received this peculiarity, according to which it is imparticipable, from something else.[49] But if it is inferior to other things, and proceeds from them, it does not proceed from them so far as it is imparticipable, but so far as it participates. For of the things from which it originates, it doubtless participates, and it is not primarily the things of which it participates. Hence, it is not from a cause so far as it is imparticipable. For so far as it is from a cause it participates, and is not imparticipable. But so far as it is imparticipable, it is the cause of things that are participated, and is not itself a participant of other things.

Proposition 100.

Every series of wholes is extended to an imparticipable cause and principle. But all imparticipables are suspended from the one principle of all things.

For if each series suffers something which is the same [or a certain sameness,] there is something in each which is the leader, and the cause of this sameness. For as all beings are from unity, so every series is from unity. But again, all imparticipable monads are referred to *the one;* because all of them are analogous to *the one.* So far therefore, as they also suffer something which is the same through an analogy to *the one,* so far a reduction of them to *the one* is effected. And so far indeed, as all of them are from *the one*, no one of these is a principle. But so far as each is imparticipable, so far each is a principle. Hence, being the principles of certain things, they are suspended from the principle of all things. For that is the principle of all things of which all things participate. All things however alone entirely participate of the first; but of other things not all, but certain things participate. Hence also that [*i.e.* the ineffable] is simply the first, but other things are first, with reference to a certain thing, but simply are not firsts.

Proposition 101.

Imparticipable intellect is the leader of all things that participate of intellect, imparticipable life of all things that participate of life, and imparticipable being of all things that participate of being. But of these, being is prior to life, but life is prior to intellect.

For because in each series of beings, imparticipables are prior to things which are participated, it is necessary that intellect should be prior to intellectuals, that life should be prior to vital natures, and that being itself should be prior to beings. Because however, that which is the cause of a greater number of effects, precedes that which is the cause of a less number, hence, among these, being will be the first; for it is present with all things to which life and intellect are present. For every thing that lives and participates of intelligence necessarily *is;* but not vice versa. For many beings neither live, nor energize intellectually.[50] But life is the second. For all things that participate of intellect, participate also of life, but not vice versa. For many things live indeed, but are left destitute of knowledge. And intellect is the third. For every thing which is in any manner whatever gnostic, also lives and is. If therefore being is the cause of a greater number of effects, but life of a less number, and intellect of still fewer effects, being is the first, life the second, and intellect the third.

Proposition 102.

All beings which exist in any manner whatever, consist of bound and the infinite through that which is primarily being. But all living beings are motive of themselves through the first life. And all gnostic beings participate of knowledge, through the first intellect.

For if that which is imparticipable in each series imparts its own peculiarity to all the natures under the same series, it is evident that the first being also imparts to all things bound, and at the same time infinity, since it is itself primarily mixed from these. Life also imparts to all things the motion which it possesses in itself. For life is the first progression and motion from the stable hypostasis of being. And intellect imparts knowledge to all things. For the summit of all knowledge is in intellect. And intellect is the first gnostic nature.

Proposition 103.

All things are in all, but appropriately in each.

For in being there is life and intellect; and in life, being and intellection; and in intellect being and life. But in intellect indeed, all things subsist intellectually, in life vitally, and in being, all things are truly beings. For since every thing subsists either according to cause, or according to hyparxis, or according to participation; and in the first, the rest are according to cause; in the second, the first is according to participation, but the third, according to cause; and in the third, the natures prior to it are according to participation;—this being the case, life and intellect have a prior or causal subsistence in being. Since however, each thing is characterized according to hyparxis, and neither according to cause (for cause pertains to other things, *i.e.* to effects) nor according to participation (for a thing derives that elsewhere of which it participates,)—hence in being there is truly life and intellection, essential life, and essential intellect. And in life, there is being indeed according to participation, but intellection according to cause. Each of these however, subsist there vitally. For the hyparxis is according to life. And in intellect, life and essence subsist according to participation, and each of these subsists there intellectually. For knowledge is the essence and the life of intellect.

Proposition 104.

Every thing which is primarily eternal, has both its essence and its energy eternal.

For if it primarily participates of the perpetuity of eternity, it does not partially participate of it, but entirely. For either it participates of it in energy, but not in essence. This however is impossible; since in this case, energy would be more excellent than essence. Or it participates of it according to essence, but does not participate of it according to energy. In this case however, that which is primarily eternal, and that which primarily participates of time will be the same. And time indeed, will primarily measure the essence of certain things, but eternity which is more excellent than all time, will not measure the essence of any thing, if that which is primarily eternal, is not essentially contained by eternity. Hence every thing which is primarily eternal, has both an eternal essence and energy.

Proposition 105.

Every thing immortal is perpetual; but not every thing perpetual is immortal.

For if the immortal is that which always participates of life, but that which always participates of life, participates also of being, and that which always lives, always is,—hence, every thing immortal is perpetual. But the immortal is that which is unreceptive of death, and always lives. And the perpetual is that which is unreceptive of non-being, and always is. If however, there are many beings more and less excellent than life, which are unreceptive of death, but exist always;—if this be the case, not every thing which is perpetual is immortal. That however, there are many beings not immortal, that exist always, is evident. For there are certain beings indeed, which are destitute of life, but which exist always, and are indestructible. For as being is to life, so is the perpetual to the immortal. For the life which cannot be taken away is immortal, and the being which cannot be taken away is perpetual. But being is more comprehensive than life, and therefore the perpetual is more comprehensive than the immortal.[51]

Proposition 106.

The medium of every thing which is entirely eternal both in essence and energy, and of every thing which has its essence in time, is that which is partly indeed eternal, and partly is measured by time.

For that which has its essence comprehended by time, is entirely temporal. For by a much greater priority, this will be allotted a temporal energy. But that which is entirely temporal, is in every respect dissimilar to that which is entirely eternal. But all progressions are through similars. Hence there is something between these. The medium therefore, is either that which is eternal in essence, but temporal in energy, or vice versa. This latter however, is impossible. For energy would be more excellent than essence. It remains therefore, that the medium is the former of these.

Proposition 107.

Every thing which is partly eternal, and partly temporal, is at one and the same time being and generation.

For every thing eternal is being, and that which is measured by time is generation. So that if the same thing participates of time and eternity, yet not according to the same, it will be both being and generation.

Corollary.

From these things it is evident, that generation indeed, having a temporal essence, is suspended from that which partly partakes of being, and partly of generation, participating at once of eternity and time. But this is suspended from that which is in every respect eternal. And that which is in every respect eternal, is suspended from being which is prior to the eternal.

Proposition 108.

Every thing which is partial in each order, is able to participate in a twofold respect of the monad which is in the proximately superior order, *viz.* either through its own wholeness or through that which is partial in the superior order, and coordinate with the thing according to an analogy to the whole series.

For if conversion is to all things through similitude, that which is partial in an inferior order, is dissimilar to that which is monadic and a whole in a superior order. And in short, is as that which is partial, to a whole, and as one order to another. But a partial nature is similar to a whole of the same series, through a communion of peculiarity, and to the proximately superior coordinate peculiarity through an analogous subsistence. It is evident, therefore, that through these media a conversion from one to the other is effected, as through similars to that which is similar.[52] For the one is similar as the partial to that which is partial, but the other as that which is the appropriate of the same series. But the whole of the superior series is dissimilar in both these respects.

Proposition 109.

Every[53] partial intellect participates of the unity which is above intellect and the first, both through the intellect which ranks as a whole, and through the partial unity which is coordinate with this partial intellect. Every partial soul, likewise, participates of the intellect which is a whole, through the soul which ranks as a whole, and through a partial intellect. And every partial nature of body participates of the soul which is a whole through the wholeness of nature, and a partial soul.

For every thing partial participates of the monad which is in a superior order, either through its proper wholeness, or through that which is partial in that order, and which is coordinate to the thing.

Proposition 110.

Of all the things that are arranged in each series, such as are first, and are conjoined with their monad, are able to participate of the natures which are proximately established in the superior series, through analogy. But such as are more imperfect and remote from their proper principle, are not naturally adapted to enjoy these natures.

For because such things as are first, are allied to those in a superior series, being allotted a better and more divine nature in the order to which they belong, but such things as are more imperfect proceed further from their principle, and are allotted a secondary and ministrant, but not a primary and leading progression in the whole series;—this being the case, the former are necessarily connascently conjoined to the things in a superior order; but the latter are unadapted to be conjoined with them. For all things are not of an equal dignity, though they may belong to the same order. For there is not one and the same ratio in all. But all things proceed from their proper monad, as from one, and with reference to one thing. Hence, they are not allotted the same power. But some things are able to receive proximately the participations[54] of superior natures; while others being dissimilar to them by proceeding to a greater distance from their principles, are deprived of a power of this kind.

Proposition 111.

Of every intellectual series, some things are divine intellects, receiving the participations of the Gods; but others are intellects alone. And of every psychical series, some things are intellectual souls, suspended from their proper intellects; but others are souls alone. Of all corporeal natures, likewise, some have souls supernally presiding over them, but others are natures alone, destitute of the presence of souls.

For of each series, not the whole genus is adapted to be suspended from that which is prior to itself, but that which is more perfect in it, and sufficient to be connascent with superior natures. Neither, therefore, is every intellect suspended from deity, but those intellects only which are supreme and most single. For these are allied to the divine unities. Nor do all souls participate of participable intellect,[55] but such only as are most intellectual. Nor do all corporeal natures enjoy the presence of soul, and of the soul which is participated, but those only that are more perfect, and possess in a greater degree the form of reason. And this is the mode of demonstration in all things.

Proposition 112.

Of every order those things that are first, have the form of the natures prior to them.

For the highest genera in each order, are conjoined through similitude to the natures placed above them,[56] and through the connexion and coherence of the progression of wholes. Hence, such as the superior natures are primarily, such also is the form which these highest genera are allotted, and which is allied to the nature of those in the superior order. They are also such according to the peculiarity of subsistence as are the natures prior to them.

Proposition 113.

Every divine number is unical.

For if a divine number has a precedaneous cause, *viz. the one*, just as an intellectual number has intellect, and a psychical number soul, and if multitude is every where analogous to its cause, it is evident that a divine number is unical, since *the one* is God. But this follows, since *the one* and *the good* are the same. For *the good* and God are the same. For that beyond which there is nothing, and after which all things aspire, is God. And also that from which all things proceed, and to which all things tend. But this is good. If therefore, there is a multitude of Gods, the multitude is unical. But that there is, is evident. For every principal cause is the leader of an appropriate multitude which is similar and allied to the cause.

Proposition 114.

Every God is a self-perfect unity, and every self-perfect unity is a God.

For if the number of unities is twofold, as has been before demonstrated, and some are self-perfect, but others are illuminations from the self-perfect unities, and if a divine number is allied to and connatural with *the one* and *the good*, the Gods are self-perfect unities. And vice versa, if there is a self-perfect unity it is a God. For as unity is in the most eminent degree allied to *the one*, and the self-perfect to *the good*, so likewise according to both these the self-perfect participates of the divine peculiarity and is a God. But if a God was a unity, yet not a self-perfect unity, or a self-perfect hypostasis, yet not a unity, he would be arranged in another order, on account of the mutation of the peculiarity.[57]

Proposition 115.

Every God is superessential, supervital, and superintellectual.

For if each is a self-perfect unity, but neither being, life, or intellect is a unity, but that which is united, it is evident that every God is beyond each of these. For if these differ from each other, but all are in all, each of these being all will not be one only. Farther still, if the first God is superessential, but every God is of the series of the first, so far as a God, each will be superessential. But that the first God is superessential,[58] is evident. For essence is not the same with unity, nor is to exist the same thing as to be united. If, however, these are not the same, either the first God is both these, and in this case he will not be one only, but something else besides *the one,* and will participate of unity, but will not be *the one itself;* or he is one of these. But if indeed he is essence, he will be indigent of *the one.* It is, however, impossible that *the good,* and *the first* should be indigent. Hence, he is one alone; and therefore superessential. But if each thing imparts the peculiarity of that which it is primarily to the whole series [of which it is the leader], hence, every divine number is superessential; since every principal cause produce similars prior to dissimilars. If, therefore, the first God is superessential, all the Gods will be superessential. For they will be entirely similar [to the first]. Since, however, they are also essences, they will be produced from the first essence, as the monads of essences.

Proposition 116.

Every deity except *the one* is participable.

For that *the one* is imparticipable is evident, since if it were participated, and on this account pertained to something else, it would no longer be similarly the cause of all things; both of such as are prior to to beings, and of beings themselves. But that the other unities are participated, we shall thus demonstrate. For if there is another imparticipable unity after the first, in what does it differ from *the one?* For either it subsists after the same manner as that; and how in this case is the one the second, but the other first? Or it does not subsist after the same manner. And thus one of these will be *the one itself,* but the other *one* and *not one.* This *non-one* also, if it is no hypostasis whatever, will be *one* alone. But if it is a certain other hypostasis besides *the one,* in this case *the one* will be participated by the *non-one.* And that will be a self-perfect one, which conjoins the non-one with *the one.* So that again God will be this [*viz.* the one] so far as he is God. But that which is non-one will subsist in the participation of *the one.* Every unity, therefore, which subsists after *the one* is participable, and every God is participable.

Proposition 117.

Every God is the measure of beings.

For if every God is unical, he defines and measures all the multitude of beings. For all multitudes being in their own nature indefinite, are bounded through *the one*. But that which is one being [or being characterized by *the one*] measuring and terminating the natures with which it is present, leads into bound that which according to its own power is not bounded. For the one being has the form of *the one* by participation.

But that which is uniform, or has the form of the one, recedes from indefiniteness and infinity. And by how much the more uniform it is, by so much the less[59] is it indefinite, and without measure. Every multitude of beings, therefore, is measured by the divine unities.

Proposition 118.

Every thing which is in the Gods pre-exists in them according to their peculiarities. And the peculiarity of the Gods is unical and superessential. Hence, all things are contained in them unically and superessentially.

For if every thing subsists in a three-fold manner, *viz.* either according to cause, or according to hyparxis, or according to participation, but the first number of all things is the divine number, nothing will be in the Gods according to participation, but all things will subsist in them either according to hyparxis, or according to cause. Such things, however, as they antecedently comprehend, as being the causes of all things, they antecedently comprehend in a manner appropriate to their own union. For every thing which is the leader of secondary natures causally, contains the cause of things subordinate, in a way naturally adapted to itself. All things, therefore, are in the Gods unically and superessentially.

Proposition 119.

Every God subsists according to superessential goodness, and is good neither according to participation, nor according to essence, but superessentially; since habits and essences are allotted a secondary and manifold order from the Gods.

For if the first God is *the one* and *the good*, and so far as he is *the one*, he is also *the good*, and so far as *the good*, *the one*, if this be the case, every series of the Gods has the form of *the one*, and the form of *the good*, according to one peculiarity, and each of the Gods is not a unity and goodness according to any thing else. But each so far as he is a unity, so far he is a goodness, and so far as he is a goodness, so far he is a unity. So far also as the Gods posterior to the first God proceed from the first, they have the form of *the good*, and the form of *the one*, since the first is *the one* and *the good*. But so far as all of them are Gods, they are unities and goodnesses. As, therefore, *the one* of the Gods is superessential, so likewise is their goodness, since it is nothing else than *the one*. For each of them is not any thing else than *the good*, but is good alone; as neither is each any thing else than *the one*, but is one alone.

Proposition 120.

Every God possesses in his own hyparxis a providential inspection of the whole of things. And a providential energy is primarily in the Gods.

For all other things which are posterior to the Gods, energize providentially through the participation of them. But providence is connascent with the Gods. For if to impart good to the subjects of providential energy, is the prerogative of the providential peculiarity, but all the Gods are goodnesses, either they do not impart themselves to anything, and thus nothing will be good in secondary natures. And whence will that be derived which subsists according to participation, except from those natures that primarily possess peculiarities? Or if they do impart themselves, they impart good, and in consequence of this providentially attend to all things. Providence, therefore, subsists primarily in the Gods. For where is the energy which is prior to intellect, except in superessential natures? But providence (προνοια), as the name signifies, is an energy prior to intellect (ενεργεια εστι προ νου). The Gods, therefore, from being Gods, and from being goodnesses, provide for all things, and fill all things with the goodness which is prior to intellect.

Proposition 121.

Every divine nature has indeed for its hyparxis goodness, but possesses a power which is unsubdued and at once incomprehensible by all secondary natures.

For if it providentially attends to the whole of things, there is in it a power which has dominion over the subjects of its providential energy; through which being unsubdued and uncircumscribed by all things, divine natures fill all things with, and subject all things to themselves. For every thing of a ruling nature, which is the cause of other things, and has dominion over them, rules through abundance of power, and predominates according to nature.

The first power, therefore, is in the Gods, not indeed having dominion over some things, but not over others, but equally comprehending in itself according to cause the powers of all beings, this power neither being essential, nor much less unessential; but being connascent with the hyparxis of the Gods, and superessential. Moreover, the boundaries of all knowledge, presubsist uniformly in the Gods. For through divine knowledge, which is exempt from the whole of things, all other knowledge has a subsistence; this knowledge neither being intellectual, nor much less, being a certain knowledge posterior to intellect, but being established according to the divine peculiarity above intellect. Whether, therefore, there is a divine knowledge, this knowledge is occult and uniform [or has the form of *the one*]. Or whether there is a power uncircumscribed by all things, this power is in a similar manner comprehensive of all things. Or whether there is a divine goodness, this goodness defines the hyparxis of the Gods. For if all things are in the Gods, knowledge, power, and goodness are also in them. But their hyparxis is characterised by that which is most excellent, and their hypostasis also is according to that which is best. But this is goodness.

Proposition 122.

Every thing divine provides for secondary natures, and is exempt from the subjects of its providential care, providence neither relaxing the unmingled and unical transcendency of that which is divine, nor a separate union abolishing providence.

For divine beings abiding in their unical nature, and in their own hyparxis, fill all things with the power of themselves. And every thing which is able to participate of them, enjoys the good which it is capable of receiving, according to the measures of its proper hypostasis; divine natures, in the mean time, illuminating beings with good, by their very essence, or rather prior to essence. For that which is divine being nothing else than goodness, it supplies all things with an unenvying abundance of good, by its very being, not making a distribution according to a reasoning process; but other things receiving indeed according to their desert, and divine natures according to their hyparxis. Neither, therefore, in providing for other things, do they receive a habitude, or alliance with the subjects of their providential care. For they benefit all things by being that which they are. But every thing which makes by its very essence, makes without habitude, and with an unrestrained energy. For habitude is an addition to essence. Hence also it is preternatural. Nor being separate, do they withdraw their providential care. For thus they would subvert, which it is not lawful to say, their own hyparxis, the peculiarity of which is goodness. For it is the province of goodness to extend itself to every thing which is able to participate of it. And the greatest of all things is not that which is boniform, but that which is beneficent. Either, therefore, no being will possess this beneficent nature, or the Gods will possess it prior to beings. For it is not possible that a greater good should be present with the natures that are good by participation, but a less good with those that are primarily good.

Proposition 123.

Every thing divine is itself indeed, on account of its superessential union, ineffable and unknown to all secondary natures; but it is comprehended and known by its participants. Hence, *that which is first,* is alone perfectly unknown, as being imparticipable.

For all knowledge which subsists through reasoning and language, pertains to beings, and in beings possesses the apprehension of truth. For it comes into contact with conceptions, and subsists in intellections. But the Gods are beyond all beings. Neither, therefore, is that which is divine doxastic, or the object of opinion, nor is it dianoëtic, nor intelligible. For every being is either sensible, and on this account doxastic, or truly existing being, and on this account intelligible, or it is between these, subsisting as *being* and at the same time *generation,* and on this account is dianoëtic. If, therefore, the Gods are superessential, and subsist prior to beings, there is neither any opinion of them, nor science and dianoia, nor intellection. But the nature of their peculiarities is known by the beings that are suspended from them. And this by a necessary consequence. For the differences of participants are co-divided conformably to the peculiarities of the participated natures. And neither does every thing participate of every thing; for there is no coordination of things perfectly dissimilar. Nor does any casual thing participate of that which is casual. But that which is kindred is conjoined to that which is kindred, and proceeds from that to which it is allied

Proposition 124.

Every God knows partible natures impartibly, temporal natures, without time, things which are not necessary, necessarily, mutable natures, immutably; and in short, all things in a manner more excellent than the order of the things known.

For if every thing which is with the Gods, is with them according to their peculiarity, it is evident that the knowledge in the Gods of things inferior, will not subsist according to the nature of the inferior things, but according to the exempt transcendency of the Gods. Hence, their knowledge of multiplied and passive natures, will be uniform and impassive. If, therefore, the object of knowledge is partible, divine knowledge will be impartible. If the objects that are known are mutable, the knowledge of the Gods will be immutable; if they are contingent, they will be known by the Gods necessarily; and if they are indefinite, definitely. For that which is divine, does not receive knowledge from subordinate beings, in order that thus the knowledge may be such as is the nature of the thing known. But subordinate beings become indefinite about the definite nature of the Gods, are changed about their immutability, receive passively that which is impassive in them, and temporally that which in them is without time. For it is possible for subordinate to be surpassed by more excellent natures; but it is not lawful for the Gods to receive any thing from beings inferior to themselves.

Proposition 125.

Every God, from that order from which he began to unfold himself into light, proceeds through all secondary natures, always indeed multiplying and dividing the communications of himself, but preserving the peculiarity of his own hypostasis.

For progressions being effected through diminution, first natures are every where after a manner multiplied into the decrements of secondary natures. But these proceeding according to a similitude to their producing causes receive their orderly distribution, so that the whole of that which proceeds is after a manner the same with, and different from, that which abides; through its diminution indeed, appearing to be different, but through continuity with its cause, not departing from sameness with it. But such as that which abides is among first, such is that which proceeds, among secondary natures; and thus an indissoluble communion of the series is preserved. Each of the Gods, therefore, is unfolded into light appropriately, in the orders in which he makes his evolution. But he proceeds from thence, as far as to the last of things, through the generative power of first natures. He is always, however, multiplied according to a progression from unity into multitude. But he preserves sameness in the progression, through the similitude of the things that proceed to the leader and primary cause of each series.

Proposition 126.

Every God who is nearer to *the one* is more total, but the God who is more remote from it is more partial.

For the God, who is the cause of a greater number of effects, is nearer to that which produces all things; but he who is the cause of a less number is more remote from it. And he indeed, who is the cause of a greater number of effects, is more total; but he who is the cause of a less number, is more partial. And each indeed, is a unity; but the one is greater, and the other less in power. The more partial Gods also are generated from the more total; the latter not being divided, for they are unities; nor changed in quality, for they are immoveable; nor multiplied by habitude, for they are unmingled. But they generate secondary progressions from themselves, which are the decrements of the natures prior to them, through abundance of power.

Proposition 127.

Every thing divine, is especially primarily simple, and on this account most sufficient to itself.

For that it is indeed simple, is evident from its union; since every thing divine is most unical. But a thing of this kind is transcendently simple. That it is also most sufficient to itself, may be learnt by considering that a composite nature is indigent, if not of other things to which it is external, yet of those things of which it is composed. But that which is most simple and unical, and which establishes itself in *the good*, is most sufficient to itself. Such, however, is every thing divine. Neither, therefore, is it indigent of other things, existing as goodness itself, nor of things requisite to composition, because it is unical.

Proposition 128.

Every God, when participated by natures nearer to himself, is participated without a medium; but when participated by natures more remote from himself, the participation is through a less or greater[60] number of media.

For the former through their alliance being uniform, are immediately able to participate of the divine unities; but the latter through their diminution, and extension into multitude, require other things which are more united, in order that they may participate of the unities themselves, and not of things united. For united multitude subsists between unity itself and divided multitude; being indeed able[61] to coalesce with unity, but allied in a certain respect to divided multitude, through the representation of multitude.

Proposition 129.

Every divine body is divine through a deified soul. But every soul is divine through a divine intellect. And every intellect is divine through the participation of a divine unity. And unity indeed is of itself a God; intellect is most divine; soul is divine; but body is deiform. For if every number of the Gods is above intellect, but participations are effected through kindred and similar natures, the impartible essence will primarily participate of the superessential unities. But the nature which comes into contact with generation will participate of them secondarily. And generation in the third place. Each of these likewise participates of them through the proximately superior natures. And the peculiarity of the Gods indeed proceeds, as far as to the last of things, in its participants; but through media allied to itself. For unity indeed imparts the transcendent power of itself to the first intellect, among divine natures, and causes this intellect to be like itself according to unical multitude. But through intellect it is also present with soul, conjoining soul with intellect and co-inflaming it [with divine fire], when this intellect is participable. And through the echo[62] of soul, imparting also to body its own peculiarity, if it is a body which participates something of soul. And thus body becomes not only animated and intellectual, but also divine. For it receives life indeed and motion from soul; but indissoluble permanency from intellect; and divine union from participated unity.[63] For each of these imparts its own hyparxis to the subsequent natures.

Proposition 130.

In every divine order, such things as are first, are in a greater degree exempt from the natures proximately arranged under them, than these latter are from things subsequent. And secondary natures in a greater degree adhere to their proximate superiors, than following natures to these.

For by how much more unical and total any thing is, by so much the more is it allotted a greater transcendency with respect to subsequent natures. And by how much the more diminished it is according to power, by so much the more is it connascent with the natures posterior to itself. And more elevated natures indeed are more united with their more principal causes; but inferior natures are less united with them. For it is the province of a greater power to be more exempt from subordinate, and to be more united to better natures. As on the contrary, it is the province of a diminution of power, to recede in a greater degree from more excellent, and to be co-passive with subordinate natures. And this happens to secondary, but not to first natures, in every order of things.

Proposition 131.

Every God begins his own energy from himself.

For he first exhibits the peculiarity of his presence with secondary natures, in himself; because he imparts himself to other things also according to his own exuberant plenitude. For neither is deficiency adapted to the Gods, nor fullness alone. For every thing deficient is imperfect, and not being itself perfect, it is impossible it should make another thing to be perfect. But that which is full is alone sufficient to itself, and is not yet prepared to communicate. It is necessary, therefore, that the nature which fills other things, and which extends to other things the communications of itself should be super-plenary or exuberantly full. Hence, if a divine nature fills all things from itself with the good which it contains in itself, it is exuberantly full. And if this be the case, establishing first in itself the peculiarity which it imparts to others, it will extend to them the communications of super-plenary goodness.

Proposition 132.

All the orders of the Gods are bound in union by a medium.

For all the progressions of beings are effected through similars; and much more will the orders of the Gods possess an indissoluble continuity, as subsisting uniformly, and being defined according to *the one,* which is the principal cause of their existence. The decrements, therefore, are produced unitedly, and alone according to the similitude in beings of secondary to first natures. And this, because the hyparxis of the Gods much more consists in union than the subsistence of beings. All the divine genera, therefore, are bound together by appropriate media; and first natures do not proceed into progressions perfectly different without a medium, but through the genera common to each, from which they proceed, and of which they are immediately the causes. For these congregate the extremes into one union, being spread under some things connascently, but proximately exempt from others. And they preserve the well-ordered generation of divine natures.

Proposition 133.

Every God is a beneficent unity or on unific (ενοποιος) goodness; and each, so far as a God, possesses this hyparxis. The first God, however, is simply good, and simply one. But each posterior to the first, is a certain goodness, and a certain unity.

For the divine peculiarity distinguishes the unities and goodnesses of the Gods, so that each according to a certain peculiarity of goodness, such as that of perfecting, or connectedly-containing, or defending, benefits all things. For each of these is a certain good, but not very good. But the first God pre-establishes a unical cause. Hence, that is *the good,* as giving subsistence to all goodness. For all the hyparxes of the Gods, are not together equal to *the one;* so great a transcendency is the first God allotted with respect to the multitude of the Gods.

Proposition 134.

Every divine intellect, intellectually perceives indeed, as intellect, but energizes providentially as a God.

For it is the illustrious prerogative of intellect to know beings, and to have its perfection in intellections. But it is the province of a God to energize providentially, and to fill all things with good. This communication, however, and replenishing with good, is accomplished through the union of the replenishing natures with the causes prior to themselves; which intellect, also imitating, passes into sameness with intelligibles. A divine intellect, therefore, so far as it energizes providentially, is a God; providence being established in an energy prior to intellect. Hence, as a God it imparts itself to all things; but as intellect it is not present with all things. For a divine nature extends to things into which the intellectual peculiarity does not proceed. For beings which are without intellect desire to energize providentially, and to participate of a certain good. But this is because all things indeed do not aspire after intellect, not even all such as are able to participate of it. All things, however, aspire after good, and hasten to obtain it.

Proposition 135.

Every divine unity is participated by some being immediately, or without a medium; and every deified nature is extended to one divine unity. As many also as are the participated unities, so many are the participating genera of beings.

For neither two or more unities are participated by one being. For since the peculiarities in the unities are different, must not that which is connascent with each be different also, since contact is effected through similitude? Nor is one unity participated in a divided manner by many beings. For many beings are unadapted to be conjoined with unity, and as *beings* they are unconjoined with the unity which is prior to beings, and as *many*, they are separated from unity. It is necessary, however, that the thing which participates should be partly similar to that which is participated, and partly different and dissimilar. Since, therefore, that which participates is something belonging to beings, but unity is super-essential, and according to this they are dissimilar; it is necessary that the participant should be one, in order that according to this, it may be similar to *the one* which is participated, though of these, the latter is one in such a manner as to be unity, but the former, so as to be passive to *the one*, and to be united through the participation of unity.

Proposition 136.

Every God who is more total, and arranged nearer to the first, is participated by a more total genus of beings. But the God who is more partial, and more remote from the first, is participated by a more partial genus of beings. And as being is to being, so is one divine unity to another.

For if unities are as many in number as beings, and vice versa, and one unity is participated by one being, it is evident that the order of beings proceeds according to the order of the unities, being assimilated to the order prior to beings. And more total beings indeed are connascent with more total unities; but more partial beings with more partial unities. For if this were not the case, again similars would be conjoined with dissimilars, and there would not be a distribution according to desert. These things, however, are impossible. Since from thence the one, and an appropriate measure are luminously imparted to all things, and from these proceed. Much more, therefore, will there be an order of participation in these, similars being suspended as much as possible from similars.

Proposition 137.

Every unity in conjunction with *the one* gives subsistence to the being which participates of it.

For *the one*, as it gives subsistence to all things, so likewise it is the cause of the participated unities, and of beings suspended from these unities. But the unity belonging to every being produces the peculiarity which shines forth in that particular being. And *the one* indeed is the cause of existence simply; but unity is the cause of alliance, because it is connascent with *the one*. Hence, unity is that which of itself defines the being which participates of it, and essentially exhibits in itself a superessential peculiarity. For every where, from that which is primary that which is secondary is that which it is. If, therefore, there is a certain superessential peculiarity of deity, this also belongs to the being which participates of it superessentially.

Proposition 138.

Of all the deified natures which participate of the divine peculiarity, the first and highest is *being itself*.

For if being is beyond intellect and life, as has been demonstrated, and if it is also after *the one* the cause of the greatest number of effects, being will be the highest deified nature. For it is more single than life and intellect, and is on this account entirely more venerable. But there is not any thing else prior to it except *the one*. For prior to unical multitude what else can there be except *the one*? But being is unical multitude as consisting of bound and infinity. And in short, the superessential one[64] is prior to essence. Since also in the illuminations which are imparted to secondary natures, *the one* alone extends beyond being. But being is immediately posterior to *the one*. For that which is being in capacity, but is not yet being, is nevertheless according to its own nature one. And that which follows the being that is in capacity is now being in energy. Hence, in the principles of things, non-being is immediately beyond being, as something more excellent, and no other than *the one itself*.

Proposition 139.

All things which participate of the divine unities, originate indeed from being, but end in a corporeal nature.

For being is the first of participants, but body the last; for we say that there are divine bodies. For the highest of all the genera of bodies, souls and intellects, are attributed to the Gods, that in every order, things analogous to the Gods may connect and preserve secondary natures, and that each number may be a whole, containing all things in itself, according to the whole which is in a part, and possessing prior to other things the divine peculiarity. The divine genus, therefore, subsists corporeally, psychically, and intellectually. And it is evident that all these are divine according to participation. For that which is primarily divine subsists in the unities. Hence, the participants of the divine unities originate indeed from being, but end in a corporeal nature.

Proposition 140.

All the powers of divine natures, having a supernal origin, and proceeding through appropriate media, extend as far as to the last of things, and to places about the earth.

For neither does any thing intercept these powers, and exclude them from being present with all things. For they are not in want of places and intervals, on account of their unrestrained transcendency with respect to all things, and a presence every where unmingled. Nor is that which is adapted to participate of them, prohibited from participation. But as soon as any thing is prepared for participation, they also are present, neither then approaching, nor prior to this being absent, but always possessing an invariable sameness of subsistence. If, therefore, any terrene nature is adapted to the participation of these divine powers, they are present with it, and fill all things with themselves. And indeed they are in a greater degree present with superior natures. But they are present with those of a middle nature, according to the order which they possess. And with such natures as are last, they are present in an ultimate degree. From on high, therefore, they extend themselves as far as to the last of things. Hence also, in last natures there the representations of such as are first, and *all things sympathize with all;*[65] secondary indeed, preexisting in first natures, but first natures presenting themselves to the view in such as are second. For every thing subsists in a threefold manner, either according to cause, or according to hyparxis, or according to participation.

Proposition 141.

Every providence of the Gods is twofold, one indeed being exempt from the natures for which it provides, but the other being co-arranged with them.

For some divine essences indeed, according to hyparxis, and the peculiarity of their order, are entirely expanded above the illuminated natures. But others being of the same order, provide for things subordinate that are of the same coordination; these also imitating the providential energy of the exempt Gods, and desiring to fill secondary natures with the good which they are able to impart.

Proposition 142.

The Gods are present with all things after the same manner, but all things are not after the same manner present with the Gods. But every thing participates of their presence according to its own order and power. And this is accomplished by some things uniformly, but by others manifoldly; by some things eternally, but by others according to time; and by some things incorporeally, but by others corporeally.

For it is necessary that the different participation of the same things, should become different, either from the participant, or from that which is participated. But every thing divine always possesses the same order, and is without habitude to, and unmingled with all things. It remains therefore, that the mutation must subsist from the participants, and that in these that which is not invariably the same must be found, and that at different times they are differently present with the Gods. Hence, the Gods being present with all things with invariable sameness, all things are not after the same manner present with them. But other things are present with them as far as they are able, and according to the manner in which they are present they enjoy their illuminations. For the participation is according to the measure of the presence of the divinities.

Proposition 143.

All inferior natures fail before the presence of the Gods, though that which participates of them may be adapted to participation. Every thing foreign indeed from divine light becomes far removed from it. But all things are illuminated at once by the Gods.

For divine natures are always more comprehensive and more powerful than the things which proceed from them. But the inaptitude of the participants, becomes the cause of the privation[66] of divine illumination. For this inaptitude obscures it by its own imbecility. And this being obscured, something else appears to receive dominion, not according to its own power, but according to the imbecility of the participant, which seems to rise against the divine form of the illumination.

Proposition 144.

All beings, and all the distributions of beings, extend as far in their progressions, as the orders of the Gods.

For the Gods produce beings in conjunction with themselves, nor is any thing able to subsist, and to receive measure and order external to the Gods, [or beyond their influence.] For all things are perfected through their power, and are arranged and measured by the Gods. Prior therefore to the last genera in beings, the Gods pre-exist, who also adorn these genera, and impart to them life, formation and perfection, and convert them to *the good*. In a similar manner also, the Gods are prior to the middle and first genera of beings. And all things are bound and rooted in the Gods, and through this cause are preserved. But when any thing apostatizes from, and becomes destitute of the Gods, it entirely departs into non-entity and vanishes, in consequence of being perfectly deprived of those natures by which it was contained.

Proposition 145.

The peculiarity of every divine order pervades through all secondary natures, and imparts itself to all the subordinate genera of beings.

For if beings proceed as far as the orders of the Gods extend, in every genus of beings, there is a supernally-illuminated peculiarity of the divine powers. For every thing receives from its proximate appropriate cause, the peculiarity according to which that cause is allotted its subsistence. I say for instance, if there is a certain cathartic or purifying deity, there is also a purification in souls, in animals, in plants, and in stones. And in a similar manner, if there is a guardian, a convertive, a perfective, and a vivific power. And a stone indeed participates of the divine cathartic powers a corporeal manner only. But a plant participates it still more clearly according to life. An animal possesses this form according to impulse; the rational soul rationally; intellect, intellectually; and the Gods superessentially and unically. The whole series also has the same power from one divine cause. And there is the same mode of reasoning with respect to the peculiarities of the other divine powers. For all things are suspended from the Gods. And different natures are illuminated by different Gods; every divine series extending as far as to the last of things. And some things indeed are suspended from the Gods immediately, but others through a greater or less number of media. But *all things are full*[67] *of Gods.* And whatever any thing naturally possesses, it derives from the Gods.

Proposition 146.

The ends of all the divine progressions are assimilated to their principle, preserving a circle without a beginning and without an end, through conversion to their principles.

For if every thing that has proceeded, is converted to the proper principle from which it proceeded, much more will total orders having proceeded from their summit be again converted to it. But the conversion of the end to the beginning, renders the whole order one, definite, and converging to itself, and exhibiting through the convergence, that which has the form of *the one* in the multitude.

Proposition 147.

The summits of all the divine orders are assimilated to the ends of the natures [proximately] situated above them.

For if it is necessary that there should be an uninterrupted connection of the divine progression, and that each order should be bound together by appropriate media, it is necessary that the summits of secondary should be conjoined with the terminations of first orders. But this contact is through similitude. Hence there will be a similitude of the principles of an inferior, to the ends of a [proximately] superior order.

Proposition 148.

Every divine order is united to itself in a threefold manner, from the summit which is in it, from its middle, and from its end.

For the summit possessing a power which is most single, transmits union to all the series, and unites the whole of it supernally abiding in itself. But the middle extending to both the extremes, binds together the whole order about itself; transmitting indeed, the gifts of primary divine natures, but extending the powers of such as are last, and inserting communion in all of them, and a conjunction with each other. For thus the whole order becomes one, from natures that replenish and those that are filled, converging to the middle as to a certain centre. And the end again returning to the beginning, and recalling the proceeding powers, imparts similitude and convergency to the whole order. And thus the whole order is one through the unific power of primary natures, through the connexion existing in the middle, and through the conversion of the end to the principle of the progressions.

Proposition 149.

Every multitude of the divine unities is bounded according to number.

For if this multitude is most near to *the one* it will not be infinite. For the infinite is not connascent with, but foreign from *the one*. Indeed, if multitude is of itself, or in its own nature, separated from *the one*, it is evident that infinite multitude is perfectly destitute of it. Hence it is powerless, and inefficacious. The multitude of the Gods therefore, is not infinite. Hence it has the form of *the one* and is finite, and is more finite than every other multitude. For it is nearer to *the one* than all other multitude. If therefore the principle of things was multitude, it would be necessary that what is nearer to the principle should be a greater multitude than what is more remote from it. For that which is nearer to any thing is more similar to it. Since however, that which is first is *the one*, the multitude which is conjoined with it, is a less multitude than that which is more remote from it. But the infinite is not a less, but is the greatest possible multitude.

Proposition 150.

Every thing which proceeds in the divine orders, is not naturally adapted to receive all the powers of its producing cause. Nor in short, are secondary natures able to receive all the powers of the natures prior to themselves, but the latter have certain powers exempt from things in an inferior order, and incomprehensible by the beings posterior to themselves.

For if the peculiarities of the Gods differ from each other, those of the subordinate pre-exist in the superior divinities; but those of the superior being more total, are not in the subordinate. But more excellent natures impart indeed some things to their progeny, but antecedently assume others in themselves, in an exempt manner. For it has been demonstrated that those Gods who are nearer to *the one* are more total; and those more remote from it more partial. But if the more total have powers comprehensive of the more partial, those that have a secondary and more partial order, will not comprehend the power of the more total Gods. In the superior therefore, there is something incomprehensible and uncircumscribed by the inferior orders. For each of the divine orders is truly infinite.[68] Nor is that which is infinite, as has been demonstrated,[69] infinite to itself, nor much less to things above itself, but to all the natures posterior to itself. But infinite in these last is in capacity. The infinite however, is incomprehensible by those natures to which it is infinite. Subordinate natures therefore, do not participate of all the powers which more excellent natures antecedently comprehend in themselves. For the latter are incomprehensible by the former. Hence things of a secondary nature, from their more partial subsistence, will neither possess all the powers of more excellent beings, nor will they possess the powers which they do contain after the same manner as superior natures, on account of that infinity through which the latter transcend the former.

Proposition 151.

Every thing paternal in the Gods is of a primary nature, and is pre-established in the rank of *the good*, according to all the divine orders.

For it produces the hyparxes of secondary natures, and total powers and essences, according to one ineffable transcendency. Hence also it is denominated paternal, in consequence of exhibiting the united and boniform power of *the one*, and the cause which gives subsistence to secondary natures. And according to each order of the Gods, the paternal genus ranks as the leader, producing all thivgs from itself, and adorning them, as being arranged analogous to *the good*. And of divine fathers, some are more total, but others are more partial, just as the orders themselves of the Gods, differ by the more total, and the more partial, according to the reason of cause. As many therefore, as are the progressions of the Gods, so many also are the differences of fathers. For if there is that which is analogous to *the good* in every order, it is necessary that there should be the paternal in all the orders, and that each order should proceed from the paternal union.

Proposition 152.

Every thing which is generative in the Gods, proceeds according to the infinity of divine power, multiplying itself, proceeding through all things, and transcendently exhibiting the never-failing in the progressions of secondary natures.

For to multiply things which proceed, and to produce things into progeny, from the occult comprehension in causes, of what else is it the prerogative, than of the infinite power of the Gods, through which all divine natures are filled with prolific good? For every thing which is full produces other things from itself according to a super-plenary power. The domination of power therefore is the peculiarity of generative deity, which multiplies the powers of the things generated, and renders them prolific, and excites them to generate and give subsistence to other things. For if every thing imparts the appropriate peculiarity which it possesses primarily to other things, every thing which is prolific will impart progression, and will adumbrate the infinity which is the primary leader of wholes, from which every generative power proceeds, and which in an exempt manner pours forth the ever-flowing progressions of divine natures.

Proposition 153.

[Every thing which is perfect in the Gods,[70]] is the cause of divine perfection.

For as the hypostases of beings are of one kind, but those of superessential natures of another, so likewise with respect to perfections, those of the Gods themselves according to hyparxis, are different from those of beings, which are secondary and posterior to them. And the former indeed, are self-perfect and primary, because *the good* subsists primarily in them; but the latter possess perfection according to participation. Hence the perfection of the Gods is one thing, and that of deified natures is another. The perfection however, which is primarily in the Gods, is not only the cause of perfection to deified natures, but also to the Gods themselves. For if every thing so far as it is perfect, is converted to its proper principle, that which is the cause of all divine conversion, is the perfective genus of the Gods.

Proposition 154.

Every thing which is of a guardian nature in the Gods, preserves every thing in its proper order, and is uniformly exempt[71] from secondary, and established[72] in primary natures.

For if a guard immutably preserves the measure of the order of every thing, and connectedly contains all the natures that are guarded in their appropriate perfection, it will impart to all things a transcendency exempt from subordinate beings, and will firmly establish each thing unmingled, in itself, existing as the cause of undefiled purity to the natures that are guarded, and fixing them in superior beings. For every thing is perfect which adheres to primary natures, but is in itself alone, and is expanded above things subordinate.

Proposition 155.

Every thing vivific in the Gods is [a generative cause, but every generative cause is not vivific.[73]]

For a generative is more total than a vivific cause, and is nearer to the principle of all things. For generation manifests a cause which produces beings into multitude. But vivification represents to us the deity who is the supplier of all life. If therefore the former multiplies the hypostases of beings, but the latter gives subsistence to the progressions of life,—if this be the case, as being is to life, so is the generative order to the vivific series. The former therefore, will be more total, and the cause of a greater number of effects, and will on this account be nearer to the principle of all things.

Proposition 156.

Every cause of purity is comprehended in the guardian order. But on the contrary, not every thing of a guardian order is the same with the purifying genus.

For purity imparts to all the Gods the unmingled with things inferior, and the undefiled in the providence of secondary natures. But a guardian power also effects this, and contains all things in itself, and firmly inserts them in superior natures. The guardian therefore is more total than the purifying genus. For in short, the peculiarity of the guardian power, is to preserve the order of every thing the same with reference to itself, and to the natures prior and posterior to itself. But the peculiarity of purity is to keep more excellent natures exempt from such as are subordinate. These powers however primarily subsist in the Gods. For it is necessary that there should be one cause preceding that which is in all things, and in short, it is requisite that there should be uniform measures of all good, and that these should be comprehended by the Gods according to cause. For there is no good in secondary natures which does not pre-exist in the Gods. [Hence in the divinities purity is likewise a primary good, guardianship, and every thing of this kind.[74]]

Proposition 157.

Every paternal cause is the supplier of being to all things, and gives subsistence to the hyparxes of beings. But every thing which is fabricative of the production of form, exists prior to composite natures, and precedes their order, and division according to number, and is also of the same coordination with the paternal cause, in the more partial genera of things.

For each of these belongs to the order of bound; since hyparxis also, number and form, have all of them the nature of bound. Hence, in this respect they are coordinate with each other. But the demiurgic or fabricative cause indeed, produces fabrication into multitude. And the uniform, or that which has the form of *the one* supplies the progressions of beings. And the former indeed, is the artificer of form, but the latter produces essence. So far therefore, as these differ from each other, *viz.* form and being, so far also does the paternal differ from the demiurgic cause. But form is *a certain* being.[75] Hence the paternal cause is more total and causal, and is beyond the demiurgic genus, in the same manner as being is beyond form.

Proposition 158.

Every elevating cause in the Gods, differs both from a purifying cause, and from the convertive genera.

For it is evident that this cause also has necessarily a primary subsistence in the Gods; since all the causes of total good pre-exist in the divinities. But it subsists prior to the purifying cause. For the one liberates from things of a subordinate nature, but the other conjoins with more excellent natures. The elevating however, has a more partial order than the convertive cause. For every thing which converts, [is converted either to itself, or to that which is more excellent than itself.[76]] But the energy of the elevating cause is characterized by a conversion to that which is more excellent, as leading that which is converted to a superior and more divine cause.

Proposition 159.

Every order of the Gods consists of the first principles, bound and infinity. But one order is in a greater degree derived from bound, and another from infinity.

For every order proceeds from both these, because the communications of first causes pervade through all secondary natures. But in some things bound predominates in the mixture [of bound and infinity,] and in others infinity. And thus the genus which has the form of bound has its completion, in which the prerogatives of bound have dominion. This too is the case with the genus which has the form of the infinite, and in which the properties of infinity predominate.

Proposition 160.

Concerning Intellect.

Every divine intellect is uniform, or has the form of *the one,* and is perfect. And the first intellect subsists from itself, and produces other intellects

For if it is a God it is filled with divine unities, and is uniform. But if this be the case, it is also perfect, being full of divine goodness. And if this be admitted, it is likewise primarily intellect, as being united to the Gods. But being primarily intellect, it also gives an hypostasis to other intellects. For all secondary natures obtain their hyparxis from such as have a primary subsistence.

Proposition 161.

Every thing which is truly being, and is suspended from the Gods, is divine and imparticipable.

For since that which is truly being, is the first of the natures that participate of the divine union, it likewise fills intellect from itself. For intellect is being, as replete with being, and is therefore a divine intelligible. And so far indeed as it is deified it is divine, but as filling intellect, and being participated by it, it is intelligible. Intellect also is being, on account of that which is primarily being. But that which is primarily being itself is separate from intellect; because intellect is posterior to being. But imparticipables subsist prior to things which are participated. Hence being which subsists by itself and is imparticipable, is prior to the being which is conjoined with intellect. For it is intelligible, not as co-arranged with intellect, but as perfecting intellect in an exempt manner, because it imparts being to it, and fills it with truly existing essence.

Proposition 162.

Every multitude of unities which illuminates truly existing being, is occult and intelligible; occult indeed, as being conjoined with unity; but intelligible,[77] as participated by being.

For all the Gods are denominated from the things which are suspended from them; because from these it is possible to know their different hypostases, which are [of themselves] unknown. For every thing divine is of itself ineffable and unknown, as being connascent with the ineffable one. From the difference, however, of the participants it happens that the peculiarities of divine natures become known. The unities, therefore, which illuminate truly existing being are intelligible; because being, truly so called, is a divine intelligible, and imparticipable, subsisting prior to intellect. For this would not be suspended from the first Gods, unless they also possessed a primary hypostasis, and a power perfective of other Gods; since, as participants are to each other, so likewise are the hyparxes of the things that are participated.

Proposition 163.

Every multitude of unities which is participated by imparticipable[78] intellect, is intellectual.

For as intellect is to truly existing being, so are these unities to the intelligible unities. Since, therefore, the latter which illuminate being,[79] are intelligible, hence, the former which illuminate a divine and imparticipable intellect, are intellectual. Yet they are not intellectual in such a way, as if they subsisted in intellect, but as causally existing prior to intellect, and generating intellect.

Proposition 164.

Every multitude of unities which is participated by every imparticipable soul, is supermundane.

For because imparticipable soul is primarily above the world, the Gods also which are participated by it are supermundane, having the same analogy to the intellectual and intelligible Gods, which soul has to intellect, and intellect to truly existing being. As, therefore, every soul is suspended from intellect, and intellect is converted to the intelligible, thus also the supermundane are suspended from the intellectual, in the same manner as the intellectual from the intelligible Gods.

Proposition 165.

Every multitude of unities which is participated by a certain [sensible body is mundane.]

For it illuminates the parts of the world, through intellect and soul as media.[80] For intellect is not present with any mundane body without soul, nor are deity and soul conjoined without a medium; since participations are through similars. Intellect itself also according to its intelligible summit, participates of unity. These unities, therefore, are mundane, as giving completion to the whole world, and as deifying visible bodies. For each of these is divine, not on account of soul; for soul is not primarily a God. Nor on account of intellect; for intellect is not the same with *the one*. But each of these visible bodies, is animated indeed on account of soul, and moved of itself. But it possesses a perpetual sameness of subsistence, and is moved in the most excellent order, on account of intellect. It is, however, divine on account of union. And if it possesses a providential power, it possesses it through this cause.

Proposition 166.

Every intellect is either imparticipable or participable. And if participable, it is either participated by supermundane, or by mundane souls.

For imparticipable intellect having the first order, is the leader of every multitude of intellects. But of participable intellects, some illuminate supermundane and imparticipable soul, but others the mundane soul. For the mundane multitude is not immediately derived from the imparticipable; since progressions are through similars. But that which is separate from the world, is more similar to the imparticipable, than that which is divided about it. Nor has a supermundane multitude alone a subsistence, but there are also mundane intellects; since there is likewise a mundane multitude of Gods, and the world itself is animated, and at the same time intellectual. The participation also of the supermundane Gods by mundane souls, is through mundane intellects as the media.

Proposition 167.

Every intellect intellectually perceives itself. But the first intellect indeed, perceives itself alone; and in this, intellect and the intelligible are one in number. But each of the subsequent intellects, perceives itself, and the natures prior to itself. And the intelligible to each of these,[81] is partly that which it is, and partly that from which it is derived.

For every intellect, either[82] intellectually perceives itself, or that which is above, or that which is posterior to itself. But if indeed it perceives that which is posterior to itself, it will through intellect be converted to that which is less excellent than itself; and thus will not know that to which it is converted, as not being in itself, but external to itself. But it will only know the image of this thing, as being generated in itself from it. For it knows that which it possesses, and the manner in which it is affected, but not that which it does not possess, and by which it is not affected.

But if it perceives that which is above itself, if indeed, this is accomplished through the knowledge of itself, it will at one and the same time both know itself and that superior nature. But if it knows that alone, it will be ignorant of itself, though it is intellect. In short, by knowing that which is prior to itself, it will know that it is a cause, and will also know the things of which it is the cause. For if it is ignorant of these, it will likewise be ignorant of that which is the cause of them; not knowing that which produces what it produces, by its very being, and what the things are which it does produce. Hence, by knowing the things of which it is the cause, it will also know itself, as deriving its subsistence from thence. By knowing, therefore, that which is prior to itself, it will likewise entirely know itself. Hence, if there is a certain intelligible intellect, this by knowing itself, will also know the intelligible, being itself intelligible. But each of the intellects posterior to this, will intellectually perceive the intelligible which is in itself, and at the same time that which is prior to itself. Hence, in intellect there is the intelligible, and in the intelligible intellect. But one intellect is the same with the intelligible; and another is the same with the intelligible which is in itself, but is not the same with the intelligible prior to itself. For that which is simply intelligible is one thing, and the intelligible in that which intellectually perceives is another.

Proposition 168.

Every intellect knows in energy that which it intellectually perceives, and it is not the peculiarity of one part of it to perceive, and of another to perceive that it perceives.

For if it is intellect in energy, and perceives itself as not any thing different from the object of intellectual perception, it will know itself, and see itself. But seeing that which perceives intellectually, and knowing that which sees, it will know that it is intellect in energy. But knowing this, it will know that it perceives intellectually, and will not alone know the objects of its intellection. Hence, it will at once both know the intelligible, and that it intellectually perceives it, and by intellection it will be intellectually perceived by itself.

Proposition 169.

Every intellect has its essence, power and energy in eternity.

For if it intellectually perceives itself, and intellect is the same with the intelligible, intelligence also is the same with intellect and the intelligible. For being the medium between that which intellectually perceives, and the object of intellectual perception, and these being the same, intelligence also will be the same with both. Moreover, that the essence of intellect is eternal, is evident.[83] For the whole of it subsists at once. And this being the case, intelligence also will be eternal, since it is the same with the essence of intellect. But if intellect is eternal,[84] it will not be measured by time, neither according to its being, nor its energy. But these subsisting with invariable sameness, the power also of intellect will be eternal.

Proposition 170.

Every intellect at once intellectually perceives all things. But imparticipable intellect indeed, *simply* perceives all things. And each of the intellects posterior to it perceives all things [according to one.

For if][85] every intellect establishes its essence in eternity, and together with its essence its energy, it will intellectually perceive all things at once. For to every thing which is not established in eternity, the successive objects of its perception subsist according to parts. For every thing which is successive, is in time; the successive consisting of prior and posterior, but the whole of it not existing at once. If therefore all intellects similarly perceive all things,[86] they will not differ from each other. For if they perceive all things similarly,[87] they are similarly all things, since they are the very things which they intellectually perceive. But being similarly all things, one intellect will not be imparticipable, and another not. For their essences are the same things as the objects of their intellection; since the intellection of each is the same with the being of each, and each is both intellection and essence. It remains therefore, either that each intellect does not similarly perceive all things, but one thing, or more than one, but not all things at once; or that it perceives all things according to one.[88] To assert however, that each intellect does not perceive all things, is to make intellect to be ignorant of some particular being. For if it suffers transition in its energy, and intellectually perceives, not at once, but according to prior and posterior, at the same time possessing an immoveable nature, it will be inferior to soul, which understands all things in being moved, [or in a mutable energy]; because intellect on this hypothesis, will only understand one thing by its permanent energy. It will therefore understand all things according to one. For it either intellectually perceives all things, or one thing, or all things according to the one of intellection. For in all intellects indeed, there is always an intellectual perception of all things; yet so as to bound all things in one of all. Hence there is something predominant in intellection, and the objects of intellection; since all things are at once understood as one, through the domination of one, which characterizes all things with itself.

Proposition 171.

Every intellect is an impartible essence.

For if it is without magnitude, incorporeal, [and immoveable, it is impartible. For every thing][89] which in any way whatever is partible, is either partible on account of magnitude, or multitude, or on account of energies which are borne along with the flux of time. But intellect is eternal according to all things, and is beyond bodies, and the multitude which is in it is united. It is, therefore, impartible. That intellect also is incorporeal, is manifest from its conversion to itself. For no body is converted to itself. But that it is eternal, the identity of its energy with its essence evinces. For this has been before demonstrated. And that the multitude in it is united is evident from the continuity of intellectual multitude with the divine unities. For these are the first multitude; but intellects are next to these. Hence, though every intellect is a multitude, yet it is an united multitude. For prior to that which is divided, that which is collected into profound union, and is nearer to *the one,* subsists.

Proposition 172.

Every intellect is proximately the producing cause of beings perpetual and immutable according to essence.

For every thing which is produced by an immoveable cause, is immutable according to essence. But immoveable intellect being all things eternally, and abiding in eternity, produces by its very being that which it produces. If however it always is, and is invariably the same, it always produces, and after the same manner. Hence, it is not the cause of things which sometimes have existence, and at other times not, but it is the cause of things which always exist.

Proposition 173.

Every intellect is intellectually both the things which are prior and posterior to itself.

For it is those things which are posterior to itself, according to cause, but those things which are prior to itself, according to participation. Yet it is still intellect, and is allotted an intellectual essence. [Hence it defines] all things [according to its essence];[90] both such as are according to cause, and such as are according to participation. For every thing participates of more excellent beings in such a way as it is naturally adapted to participate, and not according to their subsistence. For otherwise, they would be similarly participated by all things. Participations therefore, are according to the peculiarity and power of the participants. Hence in intellect, the natures prior to it subsist intellectually. But intellect is likewise intellectually the things posterior to itself. For it does not consist of its effects, nor does it contain these, but the causes of these in itself. But intellect is by its very being the cause of all things. And the very being of it is intellectual. Hence it contains intellectually the causes of all things. So that every intellect possesses all things intellectually, both such as are prior, and such as are posterior to it. As therefore, every intellect contains intelligibles intellectually, so likewise it contains sensibles intellectually.

Proposition 174.

Every intellect gives subsistence to things posterior to itself, by intellection, and its fabrication consists in intellection, and its intellection or intelligence, in fabrication.

For if intelligible and intellect are the same, the essence also of every intellect will be the same with the intellection in itself. But it produces that which it produces by essence, and produces according to the very being, which it is. By intellection therefore, it will produce the things which are produced. For in intellect, being and intellection are both of them one. For intellect is the same with every being which it contains. If therefore, it makes by its very being, but its very being is intellection, it makes by intellection. Intelligence also which is in energy, consists in intellection. But this is the same with the essence of intellect. And the essence of intellect consists in producing. For that which produces immovably, [always possesses] its very being [in producing. The intelligence of intellect therefore consists in fabrication or production.[91]]

Proposition 175.

Every intellect is primarily participated by those natures which are intellectual, both according to essence, and according to energy.

For it is necessary that it should either be participated by these, or by other natures, which possess indeed an intellectual essence, but do not always energize intellectually. It is however impossible that it should be participated by the latter of these. For the energy of intellect is immoveable. And hence, the natures by which it is participated, always participate of intellectual energy, which always causes the participants of it to be intellectual. For that which possesses its energy in a certain part of time, is unadapted to be conjoined with an eternal energy. But that which has perfection according to the whole of time, is the medium between every eternal energy, and that which is perfect in a certain time, as well in the mutations of energy, as in essences. For progressions are never effected without a medium, but through kindred and similar natures, both according to hypostases, and the perfections of energies. After a similar manner therefore, every intellect is primarily participated by those beings that are able to perceive intellectually, according to the whole of time, and who always energize intellectually, though their intellection is in time, and is not eternally in energy.

Corollary.

From this therefore, it is evident that it is impossible for the soul which sometimes perceives intellectually and sometimes does not, to participate proximately of intellect.

Proposition 176.

All intellectual forms are in each other, and each is at the same time separate and distinct from the rest.

For if every intellect is impartible, and the multitude which is in it is united through intellectual impartibility, all things in it will be in one, impartibles will be united to each other, and all intellectual forms will pervade through all. But if all intellectual forms subsist immaterially and incorporeally, they are unconfused with each other and separate, and each preserving its own purity, remains that which it is. The peculiar participation however of each participating in a separate manner, manifests the unconfused nature of intellectual forms. For unless the forms which are participated were distinguished separate from each other, the participants of each of them would not participate in a separate manner, but in the subordinate natures [*i.e.* in the participants] there would be, in a much greater degree, an indistinct confusion, these being according to their order of an inferior condition. For whence would there be a separation of these, if the natures which give subsistence to, and perfect them, were without distinction, and were confused together? But again the impartible hypostasis, and uniform essence of that which contains forms, evinces their united nature. For things which have their hyparxis in the impartible and the uniform, are impartibly in the same thing. For how can you divide the impartible and *the one?* Hence, they have a simultaneous subsistence, and are in each other, each wholly pervading through the whole of each, in a manner unaccompanied with interval. For that which comprehends them is not extended with interval, nor is one of them in this thing, but another elsewhere, as in that which has interval; but every thing is at once in the impartible and in one. So that all intellectual forms are in each other, and are in each other unitedly, and at the same time each is distinctly apart from each.

Corollary.

But if some one, in addition to these demonstrations, should require also examples, let him direct his attention to the theorems which exist in one soul. For all these are in the same essence, which is truly without magnitude,[92] and are united to each other. For that which is without magnitude, does not locally contain the things which are in it, but the natures which it contains are united and separated, impartibly and without interval. For the soul genuinely produces all things, and each apart from each, attracting nothing from the rest, which, unless they were always separated according to habit, would not be separated by the energy of the soul.

Proposition 177.

Every intellect being a plenitude of forms, one indeed, is comprehensive of more total, but another of more partial forms. And the superior intellects contain in a more total manner, such things as those posterior to them contain more partially. But the inferior intellects contain more partially, such things as those that are prior to them contain more totally.

For the superior intellects employ greater powers, having more the form of *the one* than secondary intellects. But the inferior intellects being more multiplied, diminish the powers which they contain. For things that are more allied to *the one,* being contracted in quantity, surpass the natures that are posterior to them. And on the contrary, things more remote from *the one,* as they are increased in quantity, are inferior to the natures that are nearer to *the one.* Hence the superior intellects, being established according to a greater power, but being less in multitude, produce the greater number of effects, according to power, through fewer things according to the quantity of forms. But the intellects posterior to them produce fewer effects through a greater number of things, according to a defect of power.[93] If therefore, the former produce a greater number of effects, through fewer things, the forms in them are more total. And if the latter produce fewer effects, through a greater number of things, the forms in them are more partial.

Corollary.

Hence it happens that the natures which are generated from

superior intellects according to one form, are produced [in a divided manner from secondary intellects[94]] according to many ideas. And again, those natures which are produced by inferior intellects through many and distinct forms, are produced by superior intellects through fewer, but more total forms. And that indeed which is a whole and common, accedes supernally to all its participants. But that which is divided and peculiar accedes from secondary intellects. Hence secondary intellects, by the more partial separation of peculiarities, accurately and subtly distinguish the formations of primary intellects.

Proposition 178.

Every intellectual form gives subsistence to eternal natures.

For if every intellectual form is eternal and immoveable, it is essentially the cause of immutable and eternal hypostases, but not of such as are generated and corrupted. So that every thing which subsists according to an intellectual form is an eternal intellectual nature. For if all forms produce things posterior to themselves by their very being, but their essence possesses an invariable sameness of subsistence, the things produced by them will also be invariably the same, and will be eternal. Hence, neither the genera which subsist from a formal cause, according to a certain time, nor corruptible natures so far as they are corruptible, have a pre-existent intellectual form. For they would be incorruptible and unbegotten, if they derived their hypostasis from intellectual forms.

Proposition 179.

Every intellectual number is bounded.

For if there is another multitude posterior to this, essentially inferior to it, and thus [more remote from *the one,* but the intellectual number is nearer to *the one*;[95]] and if that which is nearer to *the one,* is less according to quantity, but that which is more remote from it, is more according to quantity;—if this be the case, the intellectual number also will be less than every multitude posterior to it. Hence, it is not infinite. The multitude of intellects therefore, is bounded. For that which is less than a certain thing is not infinite, because the infinite, so far as infinite, is not less than any thing.

Proposition 180.

Every intellect is a whole, so far as each consists of parts, and is united to other things, and at the same time separated from them. But imparticipable intellect indeed, is simply a whole, as containing all parts in itself totally. But each partial intellect possesses the whole as in a part; and thus is all things partially.

For if a partial intellect is all things according to one, but a subsistence according to one thing is nothing else than a subsistence partially, the whole is in each of these intellects partially, being defined according to a certain one particular thing which predominates in all of them.

Proposition 181.

Every participated intellect is either divine, as being suspended from the Gods, or is intellectual only.

For if the divine and imparticipable intellect has a primary subsistence, the intellect which is allied to this, is not that which differs from it in both respects, *viz.* which is neither divine, nor imparticipable. For things which are dissimilar in both these respects, cannot be conjoined with each other. It is evident therefore, that the medium between these is partly similar to that which is primarily intellect, and partly dissimilar to it. Either[96] therefore, it is imparticipable and not divine; or it is participated and divine. But every thing imparticipable is divine, as being allotted an order in multitude analogous to *the one*. Hence, there will be a certain intellect which is divine and at the same time participated. It is necessary however that there should be [an intellect which does not participate[97]] of the divine unities, but intellectually perceives them only. For in each series, such things as are first, and which are conjoined with their monad, are able to participate of things proximately situated in a superior order. But such as are far distant from the primary monad, cannot be suspended from the natures that proximately belong to a higher order. There is therefore both [a divine intellect,[98]] and an intellect which is intellectual only; the latter indeed, being established according to an intellectual peculiarity, which it possesses from its own monad, and from imparticipable intellect; but the former subsisting according to the union which it receives from the participated monad.

Proposition 182.

Every [divine[99]] participated intellect, is participated by divine souls.

For if participation assimilates the participant to that which is participated, and renders the former connascent with the latter, it is evident that the participant of a divine intellect must be a divine soul, as being suspended from a divine intellect, and that through intellect as a medium it must participate of the deity which it contains. For deity conjoins the soul which participates of it with intellect, and binds that which is divine to that which is divine.

Proposition 183.

Every intellect which is participated indeed, but is intellectual alone, is participated by souls which are neither divine, nor subsisting in a mutation from intellect into a privation of intellect.

For neither are divine souls of this kind, nor such as participate of intellect. For souls participate of the Gods through a divine intellect, as was before demonstrated. Nor are souls which admit of mutation, of this kind. For every intellect is participated by natures which are always intellectual, both according to essence and according to energy. For this is evident from what has been before shown.

Proposition 184.

Concerning Soul.

Every soul is either divine, or is changed from intellect into a privation of intellect; or always remains as a medium between these, but is inferior to divine souls.

For if a divine intellect indeed, is participated by divine souls, but an intellectual intellect by those souls alone which are neither divine, nor receive a mutation from intelligence into a privation of intellect (for there are souls of this kind, which sometimes perceive intellectually, and sometimes do not);—if this be the case, it is evident that there are three genera of souls. And the first of these indeed, are divine. But the second are not divine, yet always participate of intellect. And the third are those, which are sometimes changed into an intellectual condition, and sometimes into a privation of intellect.

Proposition 185.

All [divine][100] souls, are indeed Gods psychically. But all those that participate of an intellectual intellect, are the perpetual attendants of the Gods. And all those that are the recipients of mutation, are sometimes only the attendants of the Gods.

For if some souls have divine light supernally shining upon them, but others are endued with perpetual intelligence, and others again only sometimes participate of this perfection;—if this be the case, the first of these will among the multitude of souls be analogous to the Gods. But the next to these, will always follow the Gods, in consequence of always energizing according to intellect, and will be suspended from divine souls, having the same relation to them as that which is intellectual,[101] to that which is divine. And the souls which sometimes energize intellectually and follow the Gods, neither participate of intellect after a manner always the same, nor are always able to be converted [to the intelligible] in conjunction with divine souls. For that which sometimes only participates of intellect, cannot by any contrivance whatever be always conjoined with the Gods.

Proposition 186.

Every soul is both an incorporeal essence, [and separate from body].[102]

For if it knows itself, but every thing which knows itself, is converted to itself, and that which is converted to itself, does not pertain to body (since every body is without conversion to itself) nor is inseparable from body, since that which is inseparable from body is not naturally adapted to revert to itself as it would thus be separated from body;—if this be the case, every soul is neither a corporeal essence, nor inseparable from body. Moreover, that the soul knows itself is evident. For if it knows the natures that are above itself, and is also naturally adapted to know itself, it will in a much greater degree know itself from the causes prior to itself.

Proposition 187.

Every soul is indestructible, and incorruptible.

For every thing which can in any way whatever be dissolved and destroyed, is either corporeal and a composite, or is allotted its hypostasis in a subject. And that indeed, which is dissolved, is corrupted as consisting of many things. But that which is naturally adapted to be in another thing, vanishes into non-entity when separated from its subject. Moreover, the soul is incorporeal, and external to every subject, subsisting in itself, and being converted to itself. Hence, it is indestructible and incorruptible.

Proposition 188.

Every soul is both life and vital.

For that to which soul accedes necessarily lives. And that which is deprived of soul, is immediately left destitute of life. Either therefore it lived through soul, or through something else, and not through soul. It is however impossible that it should have lived through something else alone. For every thing which is participated, either imparts itself, or something pertaining to itself to its participant. But if it suffers neither of these, it will not be participated. Soul however, is participated by that to which it is present. And that which participates of soul is said to be animated. If therefore that which is participated introduces life to animated natures, it is either life, or vital alone, or both life and vital. If however, it is alone vital, but not also life, it will consist of life and non-life. It will not therefore know itself, nor be converted to itself. For knowledge is life, and the gnostic power so far as it is such is vital. If therefore, there is any thing in soul without life, this will not possess essentially the power of knowing. But if soul is life alone, it will no longer participate of the intellectual life. For the participant of life is vital, and is not life alone, *i.e.* the first and imparticipable life; but the life which is posterior to this, is both vital and life. Soul however, is not imparticipable life. And hence it is at the same time both life and vital.

Proposition 189.

Every soul is self-vital.

For if it is converted to itself, but every thing which is converted to itself is self-subsistent, the soul also is self-subsistent, and produces itself. But it is likewise life and vital, and its hyparxis is according to vitality. For it imparts life by its very being to the natures to which it is present. And if the participant is adapted, it immediately becomes animated and vital, [soul in effecting this not reasoning][103] nor acting from deliberate choice, nor vivifying by cogitation and judgment, but by its very essence, and by that which it is, supplying the participant with life. Hence the being of soul is the same as *to live*. If therefore the soul possesses being from itself, and this is the same as *to live,* and it has life essentially;—if this be the case, it will impart life to itself, and will possess it from itself. And this being admitted, soul will be self-vital.

Proposition 190.

Every soul is a medium between impartible natures, and the natures which are divisible about bodies.

For if soul is self-vital and self-subsistent, and has an hyparxis separate from bodies, it is, in consequence of being more excellent than, exempt from every thing divisible about body. For the natures which are divided about bodies, are entirely inseparable from their subjects, being co-distributed with divisible bulks. They also depart from themselves, and their own impartibility, and are co-extended with bodies. And though they subsist in lives, yet these are not the lives of themselves, but of participants. Though likewise they exist in essence and in forms, yet they are not the forms of themselves, but of those things which are fashioned by forms. If therefore, soul is not these, it is a self-subsistent essence, a self-vital life, and a knowledge gnostic of itself. Hence, it is entirely separate from bodies, but is a participant of life. If however, this be the case, it also participates of essence. But it likewise participates of knowledge from other causes. It is evident therefore, that it is inferior to impartible natures, because it is filled [with life externally.][104] But if with life, it is evident that it is also externally filled with essence. For imparticipable life and imparticipable essence are prior to soul.[105] That soul however is not primarily gnostic is evident.[106] For every soul indeed, so far as soul is life, but not every soul, so far as it is soul possesses knowledge. For to certain soul while it remains soul, is ignorant of [real] beings. Soul therefore, is not primarily gnostic, nor does it possess knowledge from its very being. Hence, it has an essence secondary to those natures that are primarily, and by their very being, gnostic. Since however, the essence of soul is divided from its knowledge, soul does not belong to natures [entirely] impartible. But it has been demonstrated that neither does it rank among the natures that are divisible about bodies. Hence, it is a medium between both.

Proposition 191.

Every participable soul has indeed an eternal essence, but its energy is accompanied with time.

For either it possesses both eternally, or both temporally; or the one eternally, but the other temporally. It cannot however, possess both eternally: for it would be an impartible essence, and the nature of soul would in no respect differ from an intellectual hypostasis, *viz.* a self-motive from an immoveable nature. Nor can it possess both temporally: for thus it would be generated alone, and would neither be self-vital, nor self-subsistent. For nothing which is essentially measured by time is self-subsistent. But soul is self-subsistent. For that which is converted to itself, according to energy, is also essentially converted to itself, and proceeds from itself. It remains therefore, that every soul is partly eternal, and partly participates of time. Either therefore, it is essentially eternal, [but participates of time according to energy,[107] or vice versa. The latter however, is impossible. Hence, every participable soul, is allotted an eternal essence, but a temporal energy.

Proposition 192.

Every participable soul ranks among the number of [truly existing] beings, and is the first of generated natures.

For if it is essentially eternal, it is truly being according to its hyparxis, and always is. For that which participates of eternity, participates likewise of perpetual existence. But if it is in time according to energy, it is generated. For every thing which participates of time, since it is always becoming to be, or rising into existence, according to the prior and posterior of time, and is not at once that which it is, is wholly generated. But if every soul is in a certain respect generated according to energy, it will be the first of generated natures. For that which is in every respect generated, is more remote from eternal natures.

Proposition 193.

Every soul subsists proximately from intellect.

For if it has an immutable and eternal essence, it proceeds from an immoveable essence. For that which proceeds from a moveable essence, is essentially changed in every respect. The cause, therefore, of every soul is immoveable. But if it proximately subsists from intellect, it is perfected by, and converted to intellect. And if it participates of the knowledge which intellect imparts to the natures that are able to partake of it; (for all knowledge is derived from intellect, and all things have their progression essentially from that to which they are naturally converted)—if this be the case, every soul proceeds from intellect

Proposition 194.

Every soul contains all the forms which intellect primarily possesses.

For if it proceeds from intellect, and intellect gives subsistence to soul; and if intellect subsisting immoveable produces all things by its very being, it will also impart to soul which it fabricates, the essential reasons [or producing principles] of all things which it contains. For every thing which produces by its very being, imparts secondarily to the thing generated by it, that which it is itself primarily. The soul, therefore, contains secondarily the representations of intellectual forms.

Proposition 195.

Every soul is all things, containing indeed sensibles paradigmatically, or after the manner of an exemplar; but intelligibles iconically, or after the manner of an image.

For subsisting as a medium between impartible natures, and such as are divisible about body, it produces and gives subsistence to the latter of these, but pre-establishes in itself the causes from which it proceeds. Those things, therefore, of which it is the pre-existent cause, it antecedently comprehends paradigmatically. But it possesses according to participation, and as the progeny of first natures the causes of its subsistence. Hence it antecedently comprehends according to cause all sensible natures, and contains the immaterial productive principles of things material, the incorporeal principles of things corporeal, and without interval, the principles of things which possess interval. But it contains intelligibles and the forms of them after the manner of an image; so that it receives partibly indeed impartibles, with multiplication unical natures, and in a self-motive manner, things immoveable. Hence it is all beings, containing such as are first, according to participation, but paradigmatically such as are posterior to its own nature.

Proposition 196.

Every participable soul, primarily uses a perpetual body, which possesses an unbegotten and incorruptible hypostasis.

For if every soul is essentially eternal, and by its very being primarily animates some particular body, [it will always animate this body. For the essence of every soul is immutable]. But if this be the case, that which is animated by it is always animated, and always participates of life. That, however, which always lives, by a much greater priority always exists. But that which always is, is perpetual. Hence, that which is primarily suspended from every soul, is perpetual. But indeed every participable soul is primarily participated by a certain body, since it is participable and not imparticipable, and animates its participant by its very being. Every participated soul, therefore, uses a body which is primarily perpetual, and essentially unbegotten and incorruptible.

Proposition 197.

Every soul is an essence vital and gnostic, and a life essential and gnostic, and is knowledge, essence, and life. All things likewise subsist in it at once, the essential, the vital, and the gnostic; and all things are in all, and each is separate from the rest.

For if it is the medium between impartible forms, and those which are divided about bodies, it is neither so impartible as all intellectual natures, nor so partible as corporeal forms. Since, therefore, essences, lives and cognitions are divided in corporeal natures, these subsist in souls impartibly, unitedly, and incorporeally, and all of them exist at once, through their immateriality and impartibility. Since, likewise, in intellectual natures, all things subsist according to union, they are distinguished and divided in souls. All things, therefore, subsist together in these, and at the same time apart. But if all impartibles subsist together and in one, they pervade through each other, and if they are separate, they are again divided without confusion; so that each subsists by itself, and all are in all. For in the essence of soul there is both life and knowledge;[108] since every soul would not know itself, if the essence of it was of itself deprived of life and knowledge. And in the life of the soul there are both essence and knowledge. For unessential[109] life, and which is without knowledge, pertains to material lives, which are neither able to know themselves, nor are genuine essences. Knowledge, also, which is unessential and without life, is without subsistence. For all knowledge belongs to that which is vital, and which is of itself allotted an essence.

Proposition 198.

Every thing which participates of time, and is always moved, is measured by periods.

For since it is measured by time, the motion of it also participates of measure and bound, and proceeds according to number. But because it is always moved, and this always is not[110] eternal, but temporal, it is necessary that it should use periods. For motion indeed is a mutation from some things to others. But beings are terminated by multitude and magnitude. These, however, being bounded, there can neither be a mutation to infinity according to a right line, nor can that which is always moved, make its transitions finitely. Hence, that which is always moved, will proceed from the same to the same, and thus will proceed periodically.

Proposition 199.

Every mundane soul uses periods of its proper life, and restitutions to its former state.

For if it is measured by time, it energises transitively, and possesses a peculiar motion.[m] But every thing which is moved and participates of time, if it is perpetual, uses periods, periodically revolves, and is restored from the same things to the same. And every mundane soul possessing motion, and energizing according to time, will have periods of motions and restitutions to its pristine state. For every period of perpetual natures is *apocatastatic,* or restorative to a former condition.

Proposition 200.

Every period of soul is measured by time. The period of other souls indeed is measured by a certain time; but that of the first soul, since it is measured by time, is measured by the whole of time.

For if all motions have prior and posterior, so likewise have periods, and on this account they participate of time. That also which measures all the periods of souls is time. But if indeed there were the same periods of all souls, and they were about the same things, the time of all would be the same. If, however, the restitutions of different souls are different, the periodic time also and which restores to a pristine state, is different in different souls.

That the soul, therefore, which is primarily measured by time, is measured by the whole of time, is evident. For if time is the measure of all motion, that which is primarily moved, will entirely participate of time, and will be measured by the whole of time. For if the whole of time did not measure its first participant, it would not measure any thing else, according to the whole of itself. From these things, however, it is evident that all souls are measured by certain measures which are more partial than the whole of time. For if these souls are more partial than the soul which primarily participates of time, neither can they adapt their periods to the whole of time. The multitude of their restitutions, however, will be parts of the one period, and of the one restitution of things to their pristine state, which is effected by the soul that primarily participates of time. For a more partial participation pertains to a less power; but a more total to a greater power. Other souls, therefore, are not naturally adapted to receive the whole temporal measure according to one life, because they are allotted an order inferior to that of the soul which is first measured by time.

Proposition 201.

All divine souls have triple energies; some indeed as souls; but others as receiving a divine intellect; and others as suspended from the Gods. And they provide indeed for the whole of things as Gods; but they know all things through an intellectual life; and they move bodies through a self-moved hyparxis.

For because they psychically[112] participate of the natures situated above them, and are not simply souls, but divine souls, and are established according to an order, in the psychical extent, analogous to the Gods, they energize not only psychically, but also divinely, being allotted a deified summit of their essence, and also because they have an intellectual hypostasis, through which they are spread under intellectual essences. Hence, they not only energize divinely, but also intellectually; the former indeed according to *the one* which they contain; but the latter through an energy established according to intellect. A third energy, likewise, is present with them, according to their own hyparxis, which is motive indeed of things naturally altermotive, but is vivific of such as possess an adventitious life. For this is the proper employment of every soul; but such energies as are intellectual and providential, they possess according to participation.

Proposition 202.

All souls attending upon, and always following the Gods, are inferior to divine, but are expanded above partial souls.

For divine souls participating of intellect and deity, on which account, they are at the same time both intellectual and divine, are the leaders of other souls, just as the Gods also are the leaders of all beings. But partial souls are deprived of a suspension from intellect, in consequence of not being able to participate proximately of an intellectual essence. For they would not fall from intellectual energy, if they essentially participated of intellect, as has been before demonstrated [in Prop. 184]. Hence, the souls which always follow the Gods are of a middle condition; receiving indeed a perfect intellect, and through this surpassing partial souls, yet not being suspended from the divine unities. For the intellect which they participate is not divine.

Proposition 203.

Of every psychical multitude, divine souls indeed being greater in power than other souls, are contracted according to number. But those that always follow divine souls have a middle order among all souls, both in power and quantity. And partial souls indeed are inferior in power to the others, but proceed into a greater number.

For divine souls are more allied to *the one,* on account of their hyparxis being divine; but souls of a middle rank, through the participation of intellect; and those of the last order, are essentially dissimilar both to those of the middle, and those of the first rank. Among perpetual natures, however, those that are nearer to *the one,* are more single in number, and are more contracted in multitude, than such as are more remote from it. But such as are more remote from *the one,* are more multiplied. The powers, therefore, of superior souls are greater, and have the same ratio to those of souls in the second rank, which the divine has to the intellectual, and the intellectual to the psychical peculiarity. Inferior souls also are more in number. For that which is more remote from *the one,* is a greater, and that which is nearer to it, is a less multitude.

Proposition 204.

Every divine soul is the leader of many souls that always follow the Gods; and of a still greater number of such as sometimes receive this order.

[For if it is a divine soul] it is necessary that it should be allotted an order [which is the leader or generator[113]] of all things, and which has a primary rank among souls. For in all beings that which is divine, is the leader of wholes. It is likewise requisite that every divine soul should neither alone preside over such souls as perpetually follow the Gods, nor over those alone that are sometimes their attendants. For if any divine soul should alone preside over those that sometimes follow the Gods, how can there be a contact between these and a divine soul, since they are entirely different from it, and neither proximately participate of intellect, nor much less of the Gods. But if it only presides over those that always follow the Gods, how is it that the series proceeds as far as to these [alone]? For thus intellectual natures will be the last, and will be unprolific, and unadapted to perfect and elevate. It is necessary, therefore, that such souls as follow the Gods, and energize according to intellect, and which are elevated to intellects more partial than divine intellects, should be primarily suspended from a divine soul. But it is necessary that partial souls, and which through those that are divine as media, participate of intellect and a divine life, should be suspended from a divine soul in the second place. For through those which always participate of a more excellent condition, those that sometimes only participate of it, are perfected. And again, it is necessary that about every divine soul, there should be a greater number of those that only sometimes follow, than of those that always attend on the Gods. For the power of the monad always proceeds into multitude, according to diminution; being deficient indeed in power, but redundant in multitude. Since every soul also of those that always follow the Gods, is the leader of a greater multitude of partial souls, imitating in this a divine soul; and elevates a greater number of souls to the primary monad of the whole series. Every divine soul, therefore, is the leader of many souls that always follow the Gods, but presides over a still greater number of those that sometimes only receive this order.

Proposition 205.

Every partial soul has the same ratio to the soul under which it is essentially arranged, as the vehicle of the one to the vehicle of the other.

For if the distribution of vehicles to souls is according to nature, it is necessary that the vehicle of every partial soul should have the same ratio to the vehicle of the soul which ranks as a whole, as the essence of the one to the essence of the other. The distribution, however, is according to nature. For things which primarily participate are spontaneously conjoined with the natures which they participate. If, therefore, as a divine soul is to a divine body, so is a partial soul to a partial body, each soul essentially participating,—if this be the case, that which was at first asserted is true, that the vehicles of souls have the same ratio to each other, as the souls themselves of which they are the vehicles.

Proposition 206.

Every partial soul is able to descend infinitely into generation, and to ascend from generation to real being.

For if it sometimes follows the Gods, but sometimes falls from an extension to a divine nature, and participates of intellect and the privation of intellect, it is evident that it is alternatively conversant with generation and the Gods. For since it is not for an infinite time with the Gods, it will not for the whole of the following time be conversant with bodies. For that which has not a temporal beginning will never have an end; and that which never has an end is necessarily without a beginning. It remains, therefore, that every partial soul must make periods of ascents from, and of descents into generation, and that this must be unceasing through an infinite time. Every partial soul, therefore, is able to descend and ascend infinitely. And this never ceases to be the case with all of them.

Proposition 207.

The vehicle of every partial soul, is fabricated by an immoveable cause.

For if it is perpetually and connascently suspended from the soul that uses it,[114] being immutable according to essence, it is allotted its hypostasis from an immoveable cause. For every thing which is generated from moveable causes, is essentially changed. Moreover, every soul has a perpetual body, which primarily participates of it. Hence, the cause of a partial soul, and therefore of its vehicle,[115] is immoveable, and on this account supermundane.

Proposition 208.

The vehicle of every partial soul is immaterial, essentially indivisible, and impassive.

For if it proceeds from an immoveable fabrication, and it perpetual, it will have an immaterial and impassive hypostasis. For such things as are adapted to suffer essentially, and to be changed, are all of them material, and in consequence of subsisting differently at different times, are suspended from moveable causes. Hence, likewise, they receive an all-various mutation, being moved in conjunction with their principal causes. Moreover, that this vehicle is indivisible, is manifest. For every thing which is divided, so far as it is divided, is corrupted, in consequence of departing from the whole, and from its continuity. If, therefore, it is essentially immutable and impassive, it will be indivisible.

Proposition 209.

The vehicle of every partial soul descends indeed with the addition of more material vestments, but becomes united to the soul by an ablation of every thing material, and a recurrence to its proper form, analogous to the soul that uses it.

For this soul indeed descends irrationally, assuming irrational lives; but it ascends laying aside all the generation-producing powers, with which it was invested in its descent, and becoming [pure, returns to the pristine condition of its nature. For the vehicle[116]] imitates the lives of the souls that use it, and they being every where moved, it is moved in conjunction with them. By its circulation, likewise it represents the intellections of some souls; but the falling of others through their inclination to the realms of generation; and the purifications of others, through the circumductions which lead to an immaterial nature. For because it is vivified by the very essence of souls,[117] and is connascent with them, it is all-variously changed in conjunction with their energies; follows them every where; becomes co-passive with them; is restored to its pristine state together with them when they are purified;[118] and is elevated when they are elevated, and aspires after its own perfection. For every thing is perfected when it obtains its proper perfection.

Proposition 210.

Every connascent vehicle of the soul, always possesses both the same figure and magnitude. But it is seen to be greater and less, and of a dissimilar figure, through the additions and ablations of other bodies.

For if it derives its essence from an immoveable cause, it is evident that both its figure and its magnitude are defined by this cause, and each is immutable and invariable. Moreover, at different times it appears to be different, as likewise greater and less. Hence, through other bodies added from the material elements, and again taken away, it exhibits a different appearance both in quantity and form.

Proposition 211.

Every partial soul descending into generation descends wholly; nor does one part of it remain on high, and another part descend.

For if something pertaining to the soul remained on high in the intelligible world, it will always perceive intellectually, without transition or transitively. But if without transition, it will be intellect, and not a part of the soul, and this partial soul will proximately[119] participate of intellect. This, however, is impossible. But if it perceives intellectually with transition, from that which always [and from that which sometimes[120]] energises intellectually, one essence will be formed, This, however, also is impossible. For these always differ, as has been demonstrated. To which may be added, the absurdity resulting from supposing that the summit of the soul is always perfect, and yet does not rule over the other powers, and cause them to be perfect. Every partial soul, therefore, wholly descends.

Notes

1. The part within the brackets is wanting in the original, in which there is evidently a defect, as the stars at the end of the proportion indicate.
2. Here also the part within the brackets it wanting in the original.
3. For εαυτῳ here it is necessary to read εαυτο.
4. It is here necessary to supply the words αφ'εαυτου.
5. This is asserted by Aristotle in his Posterior Analytics.
6. In Prop. 5.
7. For τοις αιτιοις here, it is obviously necessary to read τοις αιτιατοις.
8. For ων το μεν αυτην διδωσι, it is necessary to read ων το μετ' αυτην διδωσι.
9. From the 11th Proposition.
10. From the 7th Proposition.
11. ει is wanting in the original.
12. This is asserted in the Phædrus of Plato.
13. That if an essence is inseparable from body, it is impossible that the energy proceeding from this essence should be separate from body, Aristotle also demonstrates in his treatise *On the Soul*.
14. The words within the brackets are wanting in the original, though perfectly necessary to the demonstration of the Proposition. Hence, the words ολον κινει, μερος δε κινειται, η, must be supplied.
15. For if the whole moves, the part which is moved will at the same time be motive.
16. The truth of this may be exemplified in light. Thus for instance we see many species of light; one kind emanating from the sun, another from fire and the stars, another from the moon, and another from the eyes of many animals. But this light though various, is every where similar, and discovers in its operations a unity of nature. On account of its uniformity therefore, it requires one principle and not different principles. But the sun is the only principle of all mundane light. And though there are many participants of light posterior to the solar orb, yet they scatter their uniform light, through one solar nature, property and power. But if we again seek for the principle of light in the sun, we cannot say that the solar orb is this principle; for the various parts of it diffuse many illuminations. There will therefore, be many principles. But we now require one first principle of light. And if we say that the soul of the sun generates light, we must observe that this is not effected by her psychical multiplicity, or she would diffuse different lights. Hence we must assert that she generates visible by intellectual light. But again this production does not subsist through intellectual variety, but rather through the unity of intellect which is its flower and summit. This unity is a symbol of that simple unity which is the principle of the universe. And to this principle the solar

intellect is united by its unity; and through this it becomes a God. This divine unity of the sun therefore, is the principle of the uniform light of the world, in the same manner as simple unity and goodness is the source of intelligible light to all intelligible natures.

17. The imparticipable is that which is not consubsistent with a subordinate nature. Thus imparticipable intellect is the intellect which is not consubsistent with soul, but is exempt from it. And imparticipable soul is the soul which is not consubsistent with body. And so in other things.

18. Instead of ει γαρ αγονον, it is necessary to read η γαρ αγονον.

19. The original here is both defective and incorrect. Instead therefore of τινος γενομενον υφ' ου μαχεται, I read παν δε τινος γενομενον υφ' ου μετεχεται.

20. Instead of και οτι αλλο in this place, it appears to me to be necessary to read και οτι αλλως.

21. Instead of μετ' αυτου here, it is necessary to read μετ' αυτο.

22. For παρον here, it is necessary to read παραγον.

23. Instead of προς παν here, it is necessary to read προς αιτιον.

24. Instead of πως το διακριθεν, it is necessary to read πως το μη διακριθεν.

25. For το απ' αυτου here, it is necessary to read τω απ' αυτου.

26. For το επιστρεφον, it is requisite to read το μη επιστερφον.

27. There is a defect here in the original, which may be supplied, if instead of εστι την απο της ουσιας προς εαυτο επιστρεπτικον we read ει ουν εστι κατα την απο της ουσιας ενεργειαν προς εαυτο επιστρεπτικον.

28. ουπω is omitted in the original.

29. For μεριστην εαυτου, it is requisite to read μεριστον εαυτον.

30. The truth of this reasoning may be evinced by the following considerations. Every thing which is measured by time, and such is every corporeal nature, depends on time for the perfection of its being. But time is composed of the past, present and future. And if we conceive that any one of these parts is taken away from the nature with which it is connected, that nature must immediately perish. Time therefore is so essentially and intimately united with the natures which it measures, that their being such as it is, depends on the existence of time. But time, as is evident, is perpetually flowing, and this in the most rapid manner imagination can conceive. It is evident therefore, that the natures to which it it so essential, must subsist in a manner equally transitory and flowing; since, unless they flowed in conjunction with time, they would be separated from it, and would consequently perish. Hence, at we cannot affirm with propriety of any part of time, that it *is;* since even before we can form the assertion, the present time is no more; so with respect to all corporeal natures, from their subsistence in time, before we can say they exist, they lose all identity of being.

Such then is the unreal condition of every thing existing in time, or of every thing corporeal, and entangled with matter. But this shadowy essence of body is finely unfolded by Plotinus, in the 6th book of his 3rd Ennead, as follows: "Being (says he) properly so called is neither body, nor is subject to corporeal affections; but body and its properties belong to the region of non-entity. But you will ask, how is it possible, that visible matter should possess no real being; that matter in which stones and mountains reside, the solid earth, and bodies which mutually resist; since bodies which impel each other, confess by their collision, the reality of their existence? You will likewise ask after what manner things which neither strike against, nor resist each other, which neither externally act, nor internally suffer, nor are in any respect the objects of sight, *viz.* soul and intellect, are to be reckoned true and real beings. We reply, that on the contrary, things more corpulent are more sluggish and inert, as is evident in bulky masses of earth. But whatever is less ponderous is more moveable, and the more elevated the more moveable. Hence fire, the most moveable of all the elements, flies as it were from a corporeal nature. Besides, as it appears to me, whatever is more sufficient to itself, disturbs others less and brings less inconvenience; but such things as are more ponderous and terrene, unable from their defect of being to raise themselves on high, and becoming debile and languid, strike and oppress surrounding bodies, by their falling ruin and sluggish weight. Since it is evident that bodies destitute of life, fall with molestation on any proximate substance, and more vehemently impel and pain whatever is endued with sense. On the contrary, animated beings, as participating more of entity, by how much the more of being they possess, by so much the more harmless they impinge their neighbouring bodies. Hence motion, which is a kind of life, or soul, or an imitation of life in bodies, is more present with whatever is less corpulent; as if more of body was necessarily produced where a defect of being happens in a greater degree.

"Again, it will more manifestly appear from passivity, that whatever is more corpulent is more passive; earth in a greater degree than the other elements; and the rest in a similar proportion. For some things when divided, suddenly return to their former union, when no obstacle prevents their conjunction. But from the section of a terrene body, the divided portions always remain separate, as if destitute of natural vigour, and without any inherent desire of union and consent. Hence, they are ready by every trifling impulse, to remain as they are impelled; to rush from the embraces of bound, and hasten into multitude and non-entity. So that whatever becomes corporeal in an eminent degree, as falling fast into non-entity, has but little power of recalling itself into one. And on this account ponderous and vehement concussions are attended with ruin, when by mutual rushing one thing impels another. But when debility runs against debility, the one is valid against the other, in the same manner as non-entity rushing on non-entity.

And this we think a sufficient confutation of their opinion, who only place being in the genus of body, persuaded by the testimony of impulses and concussions, and the phantasms perceived through the senses, which testify that sense is the only standard of truth. Such as these are affected in a manner similar to those in a dream, who imagine that the perceptions of sleep are true. For sense is alone the employment of the dormant soul; since as much of the soul as is merged in body, to much of it sleeps. But a true elevation, and true vigilance are a resurrection from, and not with the dull mass of body. For indeed, a resurrection with body, is only a transmigration from sleep to sleep, and from dream to dream, like a man passing in the dark from bed to bed. But that elevation is perfectly true, which entirely rises from the dead weight of bodies. For these possessing a nature repugnant to soul, possess something opposite to essence. And this is farther evident, from their generation, and their continual flowing and decay, which are properties entirely foreign from the nature of being substantial and real."

31. ποτε is omitted in the original.
32. It is necessary here to supply the word αυθυποστατων.
33. For εις το αιτιωτερον, it is necessary to read εις το αιτιατον.
34. ολον is omitted in the original.
35. *i.e.* Any thing which is not universal (το τι).
36. του οντος seems to be wanting here in the original.
37. αιτιου is omitted in the original.
38. *i.e.* As the Greek Scholiast observes in the margin of this Proposition, from the efficacious cause of that which acts, and the aptitude of that which suffers.
39. The words το ποιουν ενεργεια ον ο αυτο δυναμει, are wanting in the original.
40. The Proposition ends here in the Greek, though very erroneously; and its conclusion forms the beginning of the next Proposition, which should begin at the words εαν το οντως ον. But instead of εαν, we must read παν.
41. i.e. With natures rising into existence, or becoming to be, as opposed to the things which are, or to beings *truly* so called (τα οντως οντα).
42. Instead of παντως το οντως ον, it is doubtless necessary to read παν το οντως ον.
43. Instead of δει πρωτον εξ αμφοιν ειναι, it is necessary to read δει προ του εξ αμφοιν ειναι.
44. τι is omitted in the original.
45. After οτι, there is a chasm in the original, and the words that are wanting appear to be δε αϊδιοτης απειρια τις εστιν.
46. There is evidently a very gross error here in the original which is as follows: και γαρ εν τοις μεριστοις αι δυναμεις συναγομεναι μεν,

πολλαπλασιαζονται, μεριζομεναι δε, αμυδρουνται. For powers when congregated are not multiplied, but united. Hence it is necessary to read και γαρ εν τοις μεριστοις αι δυναμεις συναγομεναι μεν, ενιζονται, μεριζομεναι δε, πολλαπλασιαζονται, και αμυδρουνται.

47. By a strange mistake the original has απειρον here, instead of πεπερασμενον, and in the next line πεπερασμνον instead of απειρον.

48. For αιτιοις here it is necessary to read αιτιατοις.

49. Hence, as all things proceed from *the ineffable*, that which is imparticipable proceeds also from it, yet not as from a cause, but as from that which is better than cause. The procession, therefore, of the imparticipable from the ineffable is αρρητος εκφανσις, *an ineffable evolution into light*.

50. Instead of πολλα γαρ ζη μεν, ζη, και νοει, it is necessary to read πολλα γαρ οντα μεν ουδε ζη, ουδε νοει.

51. For του θανατου here, it is necessary to read του αθανατου.

52. Instead of ως δι' ομοιων ανομοιον, it is necessary to read ως δι' ομοιων εις ομοιον.

53. Instead of τως here it is necessary to read πας, and consequently the proposition is not interrogatory as in the original.

54. It is necessary here to supply the word μεθεξεις.

55. It is here requisite to supply νου.

56. For υποκειμενοις, it is necessary to read υπερκειμενοις.

57. There are two chasms in this sentence in the original, which I have endeavoured to supply in the translation.

58. That the principle of all things is something beyond intellect and being itself, was asserted by the most ancient Pythagoreans, as well as by Plato and his best disciples, as the following citations will abundantly evince.

And in the first place, this is evident from a fragment of Archytas, a most ancient Pythagorean, On the Principles of Things, preserved by Stobæus, Eclog. Phys. p. 89. and in which the following extraordinary passage occurs:

ως' αναγκα τρεις ειμεν τας αρχας, ταν τε εστω των πραγματων, και ταν μορφω, και το εξ αυτου κινατικον και αορατον δυναμει· το δε τοιουτον ον ου μονον* ειμεν δει, αλλα και νοω τι κρεσσον· νοω δε κρεσσον εστι, οπερ ονομαζομεν θεον φανερον.

i.e. "So that it is necessary to assert that there are three principles; *that which is [the subject] of things (or matter), form, and that which is of itself motive, and invisible in power*. With respect to the last of which, it is not only necessary that it should have a subsistence, *but that it should be something better than intellect*. But that which is better than intellect is evidently the same with that which we denominate god."

It must here however be observed, that by the word *god* we are not only to understand the first cause, but every god: for, according to the Pythagoric theology, every deity, considered according to the characteristic of his nature, is superior to intellectual essence. Agreeably to the above passage is that also of Brotinus, as cited by Syrianus in Arist. Meta. p. 102, b. who expressly asserts that the first cause νου παντος και ουσιας δυνεμει και πρεσβεια υπερεχει—"surpasses every intellect and essence both in power and dignity." Again, according to the same Syrianus, p. 109, b. we are informed that:

"the Pythagoreans called god the one, as the cause of union to the universe, and on account of his superiority to every being, to all life, and to all-perfect intellect. But they denominated him the measure of all things, on account of his conferring on all things through illumination, essence and bound; and containing and bounding all things by the ineffable supereminence of his nature, which is extended beyond every bound."

Των θειων ανδρων εν μεν λεγοντων τον θεον ως ενωσεως τοις ολοις αιτιον, και παντος του οντος, και πασης ζωης, και νου του παντελους επεκεινα. Μετρον δε των παντων ως πασι την ουσιαν, και το τελος επιλαμποντα, και ως παντα περιεχοντα, και οριζοντα ταις αφραστοις αυτου, και παντος υπερηπλωμεναις περατος υπεροχαις.

And again, this is confirmed by Clinius the Pythagorean, as cited by Syrianus, p. 104, it which place *præclari* is erroneously substituted for *Clinni*.

"That which is *the one*, and the *measure of all things* (says he), is not only entirely exempt from bodies, and mundane concerns, but likewise from intelligibles themselves: since he is the venerable principle of beings, the measure of intelligibles, ingenerable, eternal, and alone (μονον), possessing absolute dominion (κυριωδες), and himself manifesting himself (αυτο το εαυτο δηλουν)."

This fine passage I hare translated agreeably to the manuscript corrections of the learned Gale, the original of which he has not inserted. To this we may likewise add the testimony of Philolaus; who, as Syrianus informs us, p. 103, knew that cause which is superior to the two first elements of things, bound and infinite. For (says he):

"Philolaus asserts that the deity established bound and infinite: by bound indeed exhibiting every coordination, which is more allied to *the one;* but by infinity a nature subjected to *bound*. And prior to these two principles he places one, and a singular cause, separated from the universality of things, which Archainetus (Αρχαινετος) denominates a cause prior to cause; but which, according to Philolaus, is the principle of all things."

To all these respectable authorities for the superessential nature of the first cause, we may add the testimony of Sextus Empiricus himself. For in his books against the Mathematicians (p. 425) he informs us that "the Pythagoreans placed the one as transcending the genus of things which are essentially understood." και δη των μεν καθ' αυτα νοουμενον γενος υπεστησαντο Πυθαγορικοι παιδες, ως επαναβεβηκος το εν. In which passage, by things which are essentially understood, nothing more is meant than intelligible essences, as is obvious to every tyro in the Platonic and Pythagoric philosophy.

But in consequence of this doctrine of the ancients concerning *the one*, or the first principle of things, we may discover the meaning and propriety of those appellations given by the Pythagoreans to unity, according to Photius and others: such as αλαμπια, σκοτωδια, αμεξια, βαραθρον υποχθονιον, Απολλων, etc. viz. *obscurity, or without illumination, darkness, without mixture, a subterranean profundity, Apollo*, etc. For, considered as ineffable, incomprehensible, and superessential, he may be very properly called *obscurity, darkness,* and a *subterranean profundity;* but considered as perfectly simple and one, he may with no less propriety be denominated *without mixture*, and *Apollo;* since Apollo signifies a privation of multitude. "For (says Plotinus) the Pythagorean denominated the first God Apollo, according to a more secret signification, implying a negation of many." Ennead. 5, lib. 5. To which we may add, that the epithets *darkness* and *obscurity* wonderfully agree with the appellation of a *thrice unknown darkness*, employed by the Egyptians, according to Damascius,† in their meet mystical invocations of the first God; and at the same time afford a sufficient reason for the remarkable silence of the most ancient philosophers and poets concerning this highest and ineffable cause.

This silence is indeed remarkably obvious in Hesiod, when in his Theogony he says:

ητοι μεν πρωτιστα Χαος γενετ',————

That is, "*Chaos was the first thing which was generated*"—and consequently there must be some cause prior to Chaos, through which it was produced; for there can be no effect without a cause. Such, however, is the ignorance of the moderns, that in all the editions of Hesiod, γενετο is translated *fruit*, as if the poet had said that *Chaos was the first of all things;* and he is even accused by Cudworth on this account, as leaning to the atheistical system. But the following testimonies clearly prove, that in the opinion of all antiquity, γενετο was considered as meaning *was generated*, and not *was* simply. And in the first place, this is clearly asserted by Aristotle in lib. 3, de Carlo. "There are certain persons (says he) who assert that there is nothing unbegotten, but that all things are generated.—And this is especially the case with the followers of Hesiod."—εισι γαρ τινες οι φασιν ουθεν αγεννητον ειναι, αλλα οαντα γιγνεσθαι.—μαλιστα μεν οι περι τον Ησιοδον. And again, by Sestus Empiricus in his treatise Adversus Mathemat. p. 383, edit. Steph. who relates, that this very passage was the occasion of Epicurus applying himself to philosophy. "For (says ηe) when Epicurus was as yet but a young man, he asked a grammarian, who was reading to him this line of Hesiod,

Chaos of all things was the first produc'd,

from what Chaos was *generated*, if it was the first thing generated. And upon the grammarian replying that it was not his business to teach things of this kind, but was the province of those who are called philosophers.—To those then, says Epicurus, must I betake myself, since they know the truth of things." κομιδη γαρ μειρακισκος ων, ηρετο τον επαναγινωσκοντα αυτω Γραμματιστην (η τοι μεν πρωτιστα Χαος γενετ') εκ τινος το χαος εγενετο, ειπερ πρωτον εγεντο. Τουτου δε ειποντος μη αυτου εργον ειναι τα τοιαυτα διδασκειν, αλλα των καλουμενων φιλοσοφων· τοινυν εφησεν ο Επικουρος, επ' εκεινους μοι βαδιστεον εστιν, ειπερ αυτοι την των οντων αληθειαν ισασιν.

Simplicius too, in commenting on the passage above cited from Aristotle, beautifully observes as follows: "Aristotle (says he) ranks Hesiod among the first physiologists, because he sings Chaos was first *generated*. He says, therefore, that Hesiod in a particular manner makes all things to be generated, because that which is first is by him said to be generated. But it is probable that Aristotle calls Orpheus and Musæus the first physiologists, who assert *that all things are generated except the first*. It is, however, evident that those theologists, singing in fabulous strains, meant nothing more by *generation* than the procession of things from their causes; on which account *all of them consider the first cause as unbegotten*. For Hesiod also, when he says that *Chaos was first generated,* insinuates that there was something prior to Chaos, from which Chaos was produced. For it is always necessary that every thing which is generated should be generated from something. But this likewise is insinuated by Hesiod, that the first cause is above all knowledge and every appellation." (De Cœlo, p. 147.)

---

* Instead of ον ου μονον, which is evidently the true reading, ονομον μονον is erroneously printed in Stobæus.

† περι αρχων.

59. Instead of μαλλον here, it is necessary to read ηττον.

60. η πλειονων is omitted in the original.

61. δυναμενον is omitted in the original.

62. By the echo of soul, Proclus means that vital quality by which the soul is united to the body; and which is nothing more than the last image and shadow of the soul. The necessity of such a connecting quality will easily appear, from considering that a truly incorporeal nature, like that of soul, cannot be connected with body, without a vital medium. In consequence of this we may consider with Plotinus (Ennead. 4. lib. 4.) the animated body as resembling illuminated and heated air. And the pains and pleasures of the body will be conversant with this shadow of the soul.

63. The original here is defective: for it is ενωσιν δε θειαν, απο της μετεχο ****

εαυτου υπαρξεως μεταδιδωσι τοις εφεξης. From the version of Patricius, however, the defect may be supplied as follows: ενωσιν δε θειαν, απο της μετεχομενης εναδος. εκαστον γαρ τουτων εαυτου κ. τ. λ. This emendation is adopted in the above translation.

64. For το υπερουσιον ον, it is necessary to read το υπερουσιον εν.

65. Thus too Hippocrates, ξυρροια μια, συμπνοια μια, παντα συμπαθεα. i.e. "*there is one conflux, one conspiration, and all things sympathize with all.*" He who understands this will see that the *magic* cultivated by the ancient philosophers, is founded in a theory no less sublime than rational and true. Such a one will survey the universe as one great animal, all whose parts are in union and consent with each other; so that nothing is foreign and detached; nothing, strictly speaking, void of sympathy and life. For though various parts of the world, when considered as separated from the whole, are destitute of *peculiar* life; yet they possess some degree of animation, however inconsiderable, when viewed with relation to the universe. Life indeed may be compared to a perpetual and universal sound; and the soul of the world resembles a lyre, or sow other musical instrument, from which we may suppose this sound to be emitted. But from the unbounded diffusion as it were of the mundane soul, every thing participates of this harmonical sound, in greater or less perfection, according to the dignity of its nature. So that while life every where resounds, the most abject of beings may be said to retain a faint echo of the melody produced by the mundane lyre. It was doubtless from profoundly considering this sympathy between the mundane soul, and the parts of the world, that the ancient philosophers were enabled to procure the presence of divinity, and perform effects beyond the comprehension of the vulgar. And that this was the opinion of Plotinus, the following passage evinces: "It appears to me that the ancient wise men, who wished to procure the presence of the Gods, by fabricating statues and performing sacred rites, directed their intellectual eye to the nature of the universe, and perceived that the nature of soul was every where easy to be attracted, when a proper subject was at hard, easily passive to its influence. But every thing adapted to imitation, is readily passive, and is like a mirror able to seize a certain form, and reflect it to the view." Ennead 4. lib. 3.

66. The word στερησεως is omitted in the original.

67. For μετα δε παντα θεων, it is necessary to read μεστα δε παντα θεων.

68. There is a chasm here in the original. And it appears from the version of Patricius, that the words και γαρ απειρος εστιν οντως εκαστος, are wanting.

69. In Prop. 93.

70. The words within the brackets are wanting in the original, which I have supplied from the version of Patricius. In the Greek therefore it it neccssary to supply the words παν το τελειον εν τοις θεοις.

71. For εξηρημενων it is necessary to read εξηρημενον.

72. Here also we must read ενιδρυμενον for ενιδρυμενων.

73. The words αιτια γεννητικη, αλλ πασα αιτια γεννητικη ουκ εστι ζωογονικη, are wanting in the original.

74. The words within the brackets are wanting in the original, which I have supplied from the version of Patricius. Hence, in the printed Greek text it is necessary to supply the words, εν τοις θεοις αρα, η μεν καθαροτης εστι και πρωτως αγαθον, και η φρουρα, και παν τοιουτον.

75. For τι εν, it appears requisite to read τι ον.

76. From the version of Patricius, it it necessary to supply the words η προς εαυτον, η προς το κρειττον επιστρεφεται which are wanting in the original.

77. For νῳ here, it is necessary to read νοητον.

78. For μεθεκτου here, it is necessary to read αμεθεκτου.

79. For τον νουν, it is necessary to read το ον.

80. The original in the beginning of this proposition it both defective and erroneous. For it is at follows: παν το πληθος των εναδων των μετεχομενων υπο τινος * * * * γαρ εστι των του κοσμου μερων, και δια μεσου, και της ψυχης. From the version of Patricius, however, the defect and error may be removed by reading: παν το πληθος των εναδων των μετεχομενων υπο τινος αισθητου σωματος εγκοσμιον εστι. επιλαμπει γαρ των του κοσμου μερων, και δια μεσου νου, και της ψυχης.

81. Instead of νοητον εστι. τουτο here, it is necessary to read νοητον εστι τουτῳ.

82. For ει γαρ εαυτον νοει, πας νους, it is requisite to read ἢ γαρ εαυτον νοει πας νους.

83. δηλον is omitted in the original.

84. For ακινητος here, it is requisite to read αιωνιος.

85. From the version of Patricius, it is here necessary to supply the words καθεν. ει γαρ.

86. The word παντα is omitted in the original.

87. Here also it is requisite to supply the words ομοιως παντα νοησουσι.

88. By an intellectual perception of all things *according to one,* Proclus means a perception of all things in one. For all intellectual forms are in each; so that a perception of one, is a perception of all forms, and therefore of all things.

89. It is here necessary from the version of Patricius to supply the words και ακινητος, αμεριστος εστι. παν γαρ.

90. From the version of Patricius, it is likewise necessary to supply in this place the words κατα την αυτου ουσιαν αρα οριζει.

91. The words within the brackets are omitted in the original, but may be supplied from the version of Patricius by reading after το ειναι, as follows, αει

εχει εν τω ποιειν. η νοησις αρα εν τω ποειν.

92. αμεγεθει is omitted in the original.

93. Instead of οι δε μετ' εκεινους, δια πλειονων, ελασσω κατα την δυναμιν ουν ελλαμψιν εκεινοι, κ. λ. It is necessary to read οι δε μετ' εκεινους, δια πλεινων ελασσω, κατα την δυναμεως ελλειψιν. ει ουν εκεινοι, κ. λ.

94. It is here requisite to supply from the version of Patricius, the words εκ των δευτερων διηρημενως.

95. It is necessary here to read and supply from the version of Patricius, πορρωτερον του ενος, ο δε νεορος αριθμος εγγυτερω του ενος.

96. For ει here it is necessary to read η.

97. From the version of Patricius, it is here necessary to supply the words δει τον νουν μη μετεχοντα.

98. The words και νους θειος are omitted in the original.

99. θειος is omitted in the original.

100. θειαι is omitted in the original.

101. For των νοερων, it is necessary to read το νοερον.

102. From the version of Patricius, it is here necessary to supply the words και χωριστος τον σωματος.

103. The words ψυχης ου λογιζομενης are wanting in the original; but from the version of Patricius ought to be added.

104. Here too, the words οτι ζωης εξωθεν, are wanting in the original.

105. The original here is defective, but may be restored to the true sense by reading αλλα και ουσιας, ειπερ ζωης δηλον. προ γαρ ψυχης κ. λ. Instead of αλλα και ουσιας, ειπερ ζωης. δηλον γαρ ψυχης κ. λ.

106. Instead of οτι δε και το πρωτως ζωτικον, ουκ εστι φανερον, it is necessary to read οτι δε και το πρωτως γνωστικον ουκ εστι, φανερον.

107. It is here requisite to supply the words πατ' ενεργειαν δε του χρονου μετεχουσα.

108. The words ζωη και γνωσις are wanting in the original. And immediately after, for ου γνωσεται, it is requisite to read ου γαρ γνωσεται.

109. For ανους here, it is necessary to read ανουσιος.

110. ουχ is omitted in the original.

111. For η διακινσις, it is necessary to read ιδια κινησις.

112. For φυσικως here, it is necessary to read ψυχικως.

113. There is a chasm here in the original after the word δεχομενων, which may be supplied by reading ει γαρ θεια ηγεμονικην κ. λ. and γεννητικην must be substituted for γενικην.

114. For εξηρηται τοις χρωμενοις αυτω ψυχης, it is necessary to read εξητηταιτης χρωμενης αυτω ψυχης.

115. Instead of ωστς και η μερικη ψυχη, και το αιτιον αρα του οχηματος αυτης, it appears to me to be necessary to read ωστε και το αιτιον της μερικης ψυχης, και

αρα του οχηματος αυτης.

116. There is a chasm here in the original, which as it is not supplied in the version of Patricius I have filled up by conjecture. Hence, I have added the words καθαραν, ανατρεχει εις την αυτης αρχαιαν φυσιν. το γαρ οχημα.

117. For τας ψυχας here, it is necessary to read των ψυχων.

118. For εαυτων here, the sense as well as the version of Patricius, require that we should read εαυτης.

119. That is, not through the medium of dæmoniacal and divine souls.

120. From the version of Patricius, it is here necessary to supply the words και του ποτε νοουντος.

CPSIA information can be obtained
at www.ICGtesting.com
Printed in the USA
LVHW081041110722
723201LV00013B/540

9 781546 304630